CW00818884

A CONCISE GUIDE TO

MILITARY
TIMEPIECES
1880 - 1990

A CONCISE GUIDE TO

MILITARY
TIMEPIECES

1880-1990

Z. M. WESOLOWSKI

Windrow & Greene

DEDICATION

*This book is dedicated to my father who, for over fifty years,
has shown nothing but boundless enthusiasm in the watchmaker's art. Without his constant
help and support this guide could never have been written.*

© Windrow & Greene Ltd. 1996

This edition published in Great Britain 1996
by Windrow & Greene Ltd, 5 Gerrard Street, London W1V 7LJ

Printed and bound in Great Britain by
The Amadeus Press, Huddersfield, Yorkshire

Designed by Frank Ainscough

SELECT BIBLIOGRAPHY

Military Timepieces by Marvin E.Whitney (AWI Press)

Militär-Taschenuhren by Steffen Röhner (Callwey)

Longines by Daria Marrozi & Gianluigi Toselli (Giada)

John Harrison, Copley Medalist by Col.H.Quill RM (The Antiquarian Horological Society)

The World's Great Clocks & Watches by Cedric Jagger (Galley Press)

TM 9-1575 *Ordnance Maintenance – Wrist Watches, Pocket Watches, Stop Watches and Clocks*
(US War Department, 6 April 1945)

A CIP catalogue entry for this book is available from the British Library

ISBN 1 85915 013 6

ACKNOWLEDGEMENTS

The author wishes to record his gratitude to A.J.Marriott-Smith and Kent Sales,
for their photographic contribution and for the original concept of the book; to both
Sotheby's and Christie's, for permission to use photographs and information; to the staff of the
National Maritime Museum and the Imperial War Museum, for their invaluable contributions;
and, of course, to the many collectors and fellow horological enthusiasts who have assisted
with contributions, and to the war veterans who shared the memories and records which
were so helpful during the compilation of the book.

CONTENTS

INTRODUCTION

Before picking this book up, how many times have you glanced at your watch today in order to tell the time? The answer is probably many more times than you are consciously aware. With the sheer speed and complex integration of modern urban living, and the proliferation of technological tools and gadgets in every area of our daily lives, so watches, clocks, timetables, and schedules have become an integral part of our world. We can do very little without constant reference to them; and yet we take them for granted. Especially since the advent of quartz technology, highly accurate watches have become affordable by almost every adult and child in the Western world and beyond. It is easy to forget how recently, in historical terms, we have acquired this universal access to timekeeping. Time, measured more exactly than by the sun and the seasons, was a distinctly local and subjective matter until only about 150 years ago.

The limitations of the oldest timepiece – the sundial – are obvious; yet surviving examples of folding pocket sundials dating from the medieval period and the early 16th century remind us that even this crude device was thought worth carrying. More complex mechanisms for telling the passage of hours have been with us since ancient times, the movement of their pointers relying upon the consistent release of water or fine sand, or the consistent burning–time of wicks. Mechanical clocks date from the medieval period, and the craftsmen in metal who devised and built them achieved technically impressive results by the late 16th and 17th centuries.

There is no definitive date known for the first true appearance of the pocket watch – too many variations on the theme of the small portable clock have been identified (some with striking bells but no hands). However, we can say that by the middle years of the 18th century pocket watches, often of great sophistication and jewel–like beauty, had become the ubiquitous possessions (and visible status symbols) of every man of means. Yet however accurate a man's watch or a public clock, until the advent of railway and telegraph networks a hundred years later there was simply no means of general synchronisation; and absolute accuracy had to await the invention of the radio time signal in our own century. What was a man to check his watch against, apart from another equally fallible timepiece? Everyday timekeeping must have been a chaos of relative and cumulative error. Given the pace of life and of pre–mechanical travel, this unavoidably approximate culture of timekeeping must have been tolerable. Most people lived their lives within a single locality, and the striking of public clocks would enable at least a local consensus, sufficient for everyday arrangements.

Warfare, like civil life, was conducted at the speed of a walking man or a running horse; and we must presume that before a military operation the responsible officers would have mutually synchronised their personal watches. Even so, in officers' eyewitness accounts of 18th and early 19th century battles it is notoriously difficult to reconcile the exact timing of events. For instance, the first shots of the cannonade which opened the battle of Culloden in April 1746 were reported by various participants to have rung out at a little after noon, about one in the afternoon, about five past one, about a quarter past one, at two o'clock, and at half past two; the "probability cluster" among these reports places the event at some time between one and a quarter past. (Perhaps the most infamous example is the battle of Waterloo in June 1815, probably the most written–about battle in history; generations of historians have driven themselves distracted trying to collate the reported timings of the complex sequence of movements and attacks by three different armies, and no real consensus has ever been reached.)

There was one very specific application of timekeeping, however, where real accuracy could be a matter of life or death: and that was the science of maritime navigation. It was in this field that the need for universal accuracy gave the greatest stimulus to technological progress; and the quest for an accurate naval chronometer is the Genesis story of the military timepiece. It is a story worth retelling, from the viewpoints both of technological history and the sad failings of the human character.

When the first navigators began to traverse the globe, they knew that once out of sight of land they lost all reference points with which to determine the ship's position. Reliance had to be placed on the ability to steer an accurate compass course set by dead reckoning, but no matter how hard they tried the wind and ocean currents would conspire against them. After a few weeks at sea they might find themselves hopelessly astray, perhaps hundreds of miles away from their intended landfall. If good fortune was with them they might sight land before their provisions were exhausted; the alternative was a wretched death.

The difficulty in obtaining the ship's fix, as far as latitude was concerned, was not an issue. By careful astronomical observation of the sun or certain stars at night, coupled with mathematical calculations, the navigator could work out his north/south position. Unfortunately, similar calculations to determine the longitude – the ship's east/west position – were continuously upset by the rotation of the earth about its axis. As early as 1530 the Flemish mathematician Gemma Frisius suggested that with reference to an accurate timepiece on board ship, correct orientation of the ship's position would be possible – working on the principal that the earth rotates at a rate of one degree of longitude for every four minutes of elapsed time. However, until such a timekeeper could be invented the navigator would have to rely on the humble sand glass, which could only monitor the passage of time intervals.

Sextants and quadrants were also available, but they could only be used to compute local time, not the desired "time at a known meridian", e.g. the current time at the last port of call (the universal datum points not being established as Greenwich and GMT until 1880). Log lines also had their uses in gauging the ship's speed; but despite all these aids there was still that missing ingredient, and the navigator had to place his trust in his skill and an element of luck.

By 1598 King Philip of Spain was offering a reward to anyone who could produce a solution to the longitude quandary. The Dutch, the Venetians and the French, all concerned with the impact of the problem on their overseas trade, also offered incentives to encourage research. In England in 1675 the first serious attempts were undertaken by the newly established Royal Observatory at Greenwich to chart the longitude of cities, to perfect navigation, and to further research in astronomy; King Charles II issued his Royal Warrant to John Falmsteed as the first "Observator" (later to become the office of Astronomer Royal). A Derbyshire clergyman who had acquired an enviable reputation as an astronomer and

mathematician, Falmsteed would amass details of some 40,000 observations, publishing his work in 1719 in the form of a star register which was to become the standard for modern positional astronomy.

After the further stimulus of a naval disaster off the Scilly Isles in 1701, an Act of Parliament was passed in 1714 and the then incredible prize of £20,000 – equal to a national lottery jackpot today – was offered to "Such a person or persons as shall discover longitude". To oversee the venture the Board of Longitude was set up, assembling eminent scientists, mathematicians and horologists whose brief was to evaluate and encourage prospective candidates. Any person claiming the prize would have to demonstrate that their timekeeping system would be capable of maintaining accuracy to within three seconds per day during a voyage from Britain to the West Indies. Some savants, including the great Isaac Newton, believed that the challenge was impossible.

Pendulum clocks were already available which could surpass the criteria demanded; but they required a level base for the pendulum to swing uninterrupted. Any deviation from true would stop the clock, or make its timekeeping so erratic as to be worthless. In 1660 the Dutchman Christian Huygens had concluded by experiment that a pendulum mechanism could not survive the motion of a ship at sea.

Watches were also available, relying on an oscillating balance wheel and hair spring to achieve their timekeeping ability; but this arrangement also had its flaws, the primary drawbacks being the lack of constancy in the weight of the balance wheel, which varies in different latitudes due to the effects of gravity; in the diameter of the balance wheel, which varies due to temperature; and in the quality of the hair spring and its consequent ability to resist change in form. Even the best watches of that time were only accurate to about one or two minutes per day.

By 1726 news of the Board's prize offer had reached John Harrison, a 33–year–old horological genius, who began to consider the problem of constructing a sea clock. Growing up in Barrow, Lincolnshire, he was fascinated by clocks from childhood, but initially followed his father's trade of carpentry while simultaneously teaching himself clockmaking. By 1713 Harrison had combined his talents, building his first clock almost entirely from wood. He made two more in 1715 and 1717 before teaming up with his brother James to produce a succession of high precision clocks which, thanks to their wooden construction, required no oiling. Nor were they effected by temperature variations, as their pendulums employed Harrison's "grid iron" which activated a series of complementary metal rods to cancel out the effects of expansion. These may have been the most accurate clocks yet constructed, keeping time to within one second per month.

When Harrison was ready to divulge his own designs for a sea clock he travelled to London in 1730, and approached the Board for financial assistance. The Astronomer Royal, Edmond Halley, encouraged him to speak with the famous clockmaker George Graham. Harrison was worried

A purported portrait of John Harrison (1693-1776) by an unknown artist. Behind him is his sea clock H3; at his elbow, what might appear to be H5, his duplicate of his original deck watch H4 – the original had an ornate enamel dial with acanthus and scroll decoration, while this piece appears plain. Whichever watch the portrait is meant to represent, Harrison looks unconvincingly youthful – H4 was completed when he was 66 years of age, and H5 not until he was 79. (National Maritime Museum)

that if he revealed his ideas Graham might misappropriate them, but ten hours of discussion between them satisfied him of Graham's integrity. Graham was so impressed by Harrison's concepts that he loaned him £500 from his own pocket to get the project under way.

The trials of H1

Heartened by this support, the Harrison brothers began work on their first sea clock, which became known as H1. As funds became depleted further donations were obtained from a variety of institutions, including a predictably generous sum from the East India Company. By 1736, H1 was complete. The massive timepiece stood almost a metre square; its gear wheels were of oak and the

pinions and bushes of lignum vitae – a hard wood with excellent self–lubricating properties. Harrison satisfied himself of the clock's accuracy by comparison with Sidereal Time – a method of timekeeping through astronomy, by monitoring the apparent passage of stars across the heavens, where the time taken for the earth to make one full revolution is known to be a virtually constant 23 hours, 56 minutes and 3.4 seconds.

The Board's initial sea trials took place between Portsmouth and Lisbon on board *HMS Centurion*; H1 was kept in a wooden case suspended on springs in a gimbal frame to protect it from the motion of the ship. During the return leg, this time on *HMS Oxford*, Harrison demonstrated that the ship's position was in fact some 60 miles from where the captain believed it to be. The preliminary results looked promising; but when Harrison next met the Board he requested a further £500 in order to begin work on his next clock, which he promised would be even better and smaller than H1. An agreement was reached whereby, in exchange for the grant, Harrison was to hand over the ownership of his sea clocks to the Board.

H2, and the delay of H3

Harrison moved to London to work on H2, which indeed proved to be more compact and stronger than its predecessor – albeit at a weight of 47kg, primarily due to the replacement of the wooden parts with brass and the addition of a spring remontoire which improved accuracy by eliminating the effect of the variation in the mainspring's power as it wound down. As work progressed James quit the partnership, leaving John living in abject poverty as the grants were swallowed up by research and material costs.

H2 was completed in 1739 – but Harrison never submitted it to the Board for evaluation. He preferred to pursue his pioneering work, which was already under way in the guise of H3. A further grant from the Board was secured only by Harrison's pledge to have the clock ready within the next two years. As his work progressed he found that he could not keep his promise; and in the event the deadline was exceeded by a staggering fifteen years. It was 1756 before Harrison announced to the Board that H3 was available for sea trials. He added that another project was also undergoing development; this was to be a "deck watch" – a timepiece that would be set against the master sea clock and, while retaining accuracy, would be portable.

The triumph of H4

Harrison now employed John Jeffreys to make a pocket watch incorporating his best innovative features, amongst which was a bi-metallic balance wheel which was to greatly assist in maintaining accuracy by removing expansion problems during temperature changes. Harrison found that his pocket watch kept time beyond all expectations. Exhilarated by this breakthrough he asked Larcum Kendal, a watchmaker and a member of the Board, to make a larger version of the watch in association with Jeffreys. (Harrison's son William, now aged 27, probably assisted with the project.) This new watch became known as H4.

In 1760 Harrison supplied the Board with the long–awaited H3, presenting H4 at the same time, with the claim that while it had originally been intended only to complement his giant sea clock, its performance would nevertheless match that of H3. This must have seemed an incredible boast to the Board as they examined H4 in its silver case, measuring just 13.5 centimetres in diameter and looking like an oversized pocket watch. They were sufficiently impressed, however, to award him £500, giving him a year to make any final adjustments in preparation for sea trials the following year.

When the date of the sea trial finally came around on 18 November 1761, Harrison was so confident that he insisted on H4 being tested without H3. Regrettably, at the age of 67, Harrison was not up to the rigours of such a voyage, and his son William was nominated to travel in his place. At Portsmouth H4 was placed in the cabin of Captain Diggs aboard *HMS Deptford*, surrounded by cushions to protect it. *Deptford* had a rough passage to Jamaica – so rough that after ten days there was a radical difference of opinion over the ship's position. The captain and the navigator were still deliberating whether they were to the east or west of Madeira when William Harrison and his accompanying astronomer announced that they were almost 100 miles to the west of Madeira, and that a similar island would soon be sighted to the east. Captain Diggs was suitably impressed when William's predictions proved correct. On 21 January 1762, *HMS Deptford* arrived at Jamaica; the astronomer then set about calculating the accuracy of H4 which, despite the roughest of voyages and extremes of temperature, was established as a loss of just five seconds over the entire duration of the journey – well within the requirements for the Board's grand prize.

Enter the Reverend Maskelyne

Harrison's jubilation was to be short–lived. When the Board reconvened the astronomer's calculations were scrutinised, and it was suggested that the initial observations at Portsmouth (which were

required to ensure that H4 had been accurately set) were incorrect, and that insufficient data had been gathered during the voyage and in Jamaica. The result of the trial could therefore not be substantiated, and fresh trials would have to be arranged. However, before the Board would commit themselves to more expense they now demanded that Harrison hand over to them all his work, on the pretext that H4 might one day be lost at sea.... Harrison was devastated by what he regarded as the needless destruction of a good working relationship. The Board attempted to salvage his goodwill by giving him an advance, deductable from any prize that he might later receive.

By now one of the Board's own members, the Reverend Nevil Maskelyne, was also on the way to developing an answer to the longitude problem. Maskelyne's effective method employed the system of "lunars", whereby the distance of the moon from earth was utilised in a lengthy series of complex calculations to achieve the desired result. The Board seem to have been intent that one of their own members should accomplish the long–awaited solution; and they worked with Maskelyne to produce a series of tables to assist with the reckoning, believing this to be a more practical way forward than reliance on complex mechanical instruments.

Harrison now turned against the Board, pressing his grievances in a public campaign – with considerable success. He secured the backing of King George III in his demand for an Act of Parliament awarding him the prize, legal protection for the copyright in his designs, and an assurance that H4 would not be taken to sea again. Parliament responded with an Act offering Harrison some protection. The Board made an initial (and again deductable) payment of £5,000; but interpreted the rest of the Act harshly, insisting that two exact duplicates of H4 be made, to prove the feasibility of series production for naval issue. This ensured that many years would pass before the bulk of any prize could be paid.

Yet another sea trial of H4 was arranged, on *HMS Tartar*, with William Harrison representing his father, and in the post of verifying astronomer the Reverend Nevil Maskelyne.... They set sail from Spithead on 28 March 1764, and the navigator made accurate measurements of their position right up until their safe landfall on Barbados. The results were subsequently passed to the Board, where Maskelyne – now promoted Astronomer Royal – was appointed to evaluate them in concert with four independent mathematicians. The respected watchmaker Thomas Mudge also examined H4, and submitted a favourable technical report.

During the Board's meeting – from which Harrison was excluded – it was agreed that H4 had incurred an error of 38.4 seconds, which over the distance of the voyage amounted to an inaccuracy of 9.4 miles. This was in fact three times more accurate than the Board's highest expectations. Harrison had at last established, on the Board's own admission, that if correct principals were applied watches could keep accurate time; and the problem of longitude had been solved. Harrison wrote: "I think I may make bold to say, there is neither any mechanical or mathematical thing in the world that is more beautiful or curious in texture than this my watch or timekeeper for the longitude....I heartily thank God that I have lived so long, as in some measure to complete it."

The Board remained stubborn, maintaining that all Harrison's timekeepers, detailed drawings and two further copies of H4 must be in their possession before any question of a final award could be entertained. In 1766 the Board obtained an order instructing Harrison to hand over H1, H2 and H3, which Maskelyne took it upon himself to execute.

"By God, Harrison, I will see you righted!"

The Board gave H4 to Larcum Kendall to have a duplicate made; he completed this in two years, and it became known as K1 – which accompanied Captain Cook on his second voyage of discovery around the Pacific Ocean. Later K1 sailed with Captain Bligh on his floating greenhouse *HMS Bounty*, only to come into the hands of Fletcher Christian who, following the mutiny, took it with him to Pitcairn Island. Kendal would subsequently produce two more simplified versions, known now as K2 and K3.

Meanwhile the aged John Harrison was struggling to make further copies. With his eyesight failing, and without the original H4 to work from, his task appeared hopeless; even so, H5 was completed by the time Harrison had reached the age of 79. Once again he sought the intervention of the king, requesting that his own astronomer should test H5 at his private Royal Observatory in Richmond Park. The good–natured "Farmer George" took time to listen to Harrison's account of his treatment at the hands of the Board, declaring "These people have been cruelly treated. By God, Harrison, I will see you righted!" After six weeks of assessments the accuracy of Harrison's work was authenticated to be only 4.5 seconds out. The Board, predictably, refused to accept the results of these tests as they had not been approved by themselves.

Harrison was again faced with the task of petitioning Parliament to force the Board into conceding what was rightfully his; and on 21 July 1773, amidst uproar from the king, members of Parliament and the public, the Board of Longitude reluctantly agreed to pay the balance of £8,750, on the grounds that Harrison had devoted a lifetime's work to the cause and that he was now unlikely to comply with any of the remaining conditions. (The sum of awards received over the years in fact amounted to only £18,750.) Harrison died at his London home on 24 March 1776.

* * *

The first true military timepiece had been born. England continued to lead the way in maritime expansion and, while Harrison was the undisputed winner of the prize, he was by no means the only horologist striving to meet the criteria of the Board during the many years that the prize remained unclaimed. Others followed, improving upon the foundations laid by Harrison. Towards the end of the 18th century Pierre Le Roy, working in the company of Ferdinand Berthoud on behalf of the French Ministry of Marine, produced a detent escapement which revolutionised clockmaking and has become the essence of all true modern marine chronometers. Not only was this new breed of chronometer accurate, but it could be produced in a fraction of the time and consequently at substantially lower cost. Taking the idea of large scale production further, two rival watchmakers, John Arnold and Thomas Earnshaw, set themselves up as marine chronometer manufacturers, making the English and the French the predominant suppliers of chronometers to the major sea powers of the world.

By 1818 such advances in naval chronometry had been reached that the Royal Navy began to place chronometer watches on general issue to navigators, who until then had had to purchase their own, or else rely on Maskelyne's "lunar" system for the longitude calculations. Moving on towards the latter part of the 19th and into the 20th century, the Admiralty arranged for a series of chronometer trials which encouraged many watchmakers to submit their work for evaluation. Competition was fierce, and the advances made possible by the Industrial Revolution of the mid–19th century spawned a large number of timepieces of unprecedented veracity. Watchmakers now had the ability to mass–produce watches using the most modern of manufacturing methods. The outcome was that many watchmakers earned the right to boast their status as "Chronometer makers to the Admiralty" – a legend that is frequently seen on the dials and movements of watches.

Mass production also reduced the retail price of individual watches to such an extent that the reluctance of the British Army to issue good timepieces on grounds of cost would gradually be eroded. For many generations the military culture had asked no more of the man in the ranks than obedience; only officers had any real need to tell time accurately, and all members of the officer class would by definition be able to afford good watches. But by the late 19th century increasingly sophisticated technology dominated the world of the artilleryman, the military engineer, the signaller and the transport officer, in particular.

The wildfire spread of the railways had been a major stimulus to the production of accurate timepieces at prices allowing their issue in large numbers to responsible employees. The good watch as a necessary tool in a technical trade ceased to be a novelty among at least the elite of the working classes. Simultaneously, in Britain, the age of army reforms instituted by Edward Cardwell from the beginning of the 1870s was improving the skills, career prospects, and expectations of at least the more ambitious soldiers of the long–service professional army; and in continental European armies a system of universal military conscription for training and reserve service raised the average educational standards in the ranks. The turn of the century, with its bolt–action rifles and belt–fed machine–guns, put more complex machinery than ever before into the hands of even the private of infantry – let alone the gunner serving sophisticated breech–loading artillery. The "scientific" army was at least on the horizon.

It was the First World War, with its frantic pace of military innovation and the vast scope of its operations, which completed the process. It was a war fought – after the first few months – by soldiers conscripted from every level of an increasingly educated society, in vast numbers, mobilised, transported, supplied and deployed on a previously unimaginable scale. The days when a timepiece had been the prerogative of the navigator alone were now forgotten; it was now within the reach of – and might be an absolute necessity for – many soldiers, some sailors, and all airmen to be issued with one. Communications, mechanical transport, military flying, sophisticated munitions and their exact application – all would leap ahead during those few terrible years; and the need for accurate co–ordination of timing was basic to the whole exercise. Military service would put watches into the pockets, and later onto the wrists, of men who could never have afforded them in civil life. (It should be remembered that even in the 1940s a good wristwatch was still a desirable enough novelty to be a favourite item of personal loot among the soldiers of all armies.)

Horology has progressed throughout the past century – and particularly during the two World Wars – largely in response to military necessity. Many of the attributes of good commercial watches – accuracy, interval timing, luminous dials, shockproofing, waterproofing, and temperature tolerance – can be traced directly to the demands of the military. The resulting clocks and watches have the distinction of being the most complicated pieces of equipment ever to have been issued to individuals in the ranks of the armed forces.

*   *   *

There is no need here to persuade the reader of the fascination of horology as a whole – if you have bought this book and read this far, you are presumably among the converted. But the study and collection of military timepieces has a special appeal, which we hope this first book on the subject may convey to some degree. There is the satisfaction of correlating their technical features with the particular practical demands with which war confronted the men and women who wore them. There is the pleasure of the detective work which their myriad of manufacturers' and government markings allows. And there is the special romance which – for good or ill – attaches to all historical military collectables.

In these pages the reader will find timepieces which were used by the crews of First World War Zeppelin airships, and by the first generation of fighter pilots who hunted them; by the officers and men whose ordeal in the trenches of 1915–18 changed warfare forever; by the Tommies, GIs and Marines of 1939–45; by the crews of Admiral Doenitz's U–boats, and of the anti–submarine escort ships of Churchill's Royal Navy; by a Heinkel squadron which fought in the Battle of Britain, and by Japanese Navy aircrew of the Pacific War; by Italy's elite frogmen of 1940–43, and their US Navy counterparts of 1943–45; by post–war nuclear bomber and submarine crews, and by today's Special Forces. Each of them, by association, carries a little echo of some of the most dramatic events of our century.

GUIDE TO MILITARY TIMEPIECE MARKINGS

GREAT BRITAIN

The broad arrow British government property mark, found in various forms on watch dials, cases and movements.

C ↑ W   Chronometer Watch mark found on deck watch transit cases.

A ↑ D   Admiralty Department issue pocket watch mark, c.1914.

A ↑ S   Royal Naval Air Service issue pocket watch mark, c.1914.

ADMIRALTY MARK II A↑D   Mark II Royal Naval Air Service aviator's eight-day pocket watch, c.1914.

H. S.   Hydrographic Service mark found on the cases of Royal Navy issue watches, 1914-1918.

Numbered Hydrographic Service codes used by Royal Navy, 1939-1946, to identify the grade or use of timepieces:

H ↑ S 1   Chronometer watch with detent escapement.

H ↑ S 2   Chronometer watch adjusted for isochronism in five positions.

H ↑ S 3   Deck watch adjusted for isochronism in a minimum of two positions.

H ↑ S 4   Fleet Air Arm instrument panel watch.

H ↑ S 5   Survey boat pocket watch.

H ↑ S 6   Ship's chronometer with gimballed movement.

H ↑ S 7   Watch calibrated for sidereal time.

H ↑ S 8   Fleet Air Arm pilot's wristwatch.

H ↑ S 9   Chronograph wristwatch.

H ↑ S 10   Diver's wristwatch.

H ↑ S 11   Standard issue wristwatch.

0552 -   Stores prefix for Royal Navy NATO issue watch.

British Army issue pocket watch in India, c.1900.

W ↑ D   War Department issue pocket watch, c.1914.

51714F   Broad arrow and serial number of H.Williamson issue pocket watch, c.1914.

8173IC R A   Royal Artillery issue pocket watch with contract number, c.1914.

P↑W   Pocket watch mark, Royal Navy issue, c.1914.

↑ TW   "Tank Watch" mark found on economy grade Ingersol issue pocket watch, c.1920

6645-   NATO stores code for military wristwatch.

P   Phosphorous painted watch dial mark.

T   Tritium painted watch dial mark.

A ↑   Aviation issue mark – Royal Flying Corps pocket watch, 1914-1917.

MARK IV.A   Mark IV.A pattern mark on aviator's issue eight-day pocket watch, c.1914.

8 DAY NON LUMINOUS MARK V	Mark V pattern mark on aviator's issue eight-day pocket watch, c.1916.
30 HOUR NON LUMINOUS MARK V	Mark V pattern mark on aviator's issue standard pocket watch, c.1916.
30 HOUR LUMINOUS MARK V	Mark V pattern mark on aviator's issue pocket watch, c.1916.
R.A.E. REPAIR	Royal Aircraft Establishment repair mark to watch, pre-1917.
R.A.F. REPAIR	Royal Air Force repair mark to watch, post-1918
MU 23	Maintenance Unit repair mark hand-painted on clock dial, c.1939.
[RAF crest]	Royal Air Force crest found on clock dials, c.1937-1945.
90260 C ↑	Contract number on Army issue wristwatch, c.1918.
W.9019.S	Wristwatch, Service pattern mark flanking issue number, c.1918.
↑ 94455M ✕	Service cancellation mark added in the 1930s to a military issue wristwatch of c.1918.
Mk I ↑	Highest grade Army issue pocket watch mark, c.1925.
s↑s	Service wristwatch mark, Indian Army, c.1930.
C.S.(I)	Civil Service (India) mark on military issue wristwatch, c.1939.
↑ G.S. M.K.II	General Service Mark II pocket watch mark, Army issue, c.1935
↑ GS/TP	General Service Timepiece/Temporary Pattern mark, Army issue,1939-1945.
↑ G.S.T.P.	Variation on above.
↑ ATP	Army Time Piece mark found on wristwatches, 1939-1945.
C.O.S.D	Company Ordnance Supply Depot mark found on Airborne Forces issue wristwatch, c.1944.
W.W.W.	Wrist Watch, Waterproof mark used on military contract watches, c.1943-1958.
W10-	Army prefix to wristwatch serial number, post-1950.
[crown] A·M·	Air Ministry property stamp found in various forms on watches, clocks and their movements, 1918-c.1953.
A.M. 6B/107	Air Ministry flying equipment code for split chronograph watch, c.1937.
A.M. 6B/117	Air Ministry issue code for stop watch, c.1940.
A.M. 6B/159 G & S Co. Ltd. 8435/40	Air Ministry issue code for a pilot's/navigator's watch, in this case supplied by the Goldsmith's & Silversmith's Company Limited, bearing issue number and dated 1940.
A.M. 6B/221	Air Ministry issue code for substitute standard stop watch, c.1942.
A.M. 6B/234	Air Ministry issue code for substitute standard pilot's wristwatch. Mark also follows repair/reissue 1939-1945.
A.M. 14.A/1102 21887	Air Ministry issue code found on wristwatch used for reconnaissance/ground operations duty, c.1940.
A.M. 6E/ 50	Air Ministry issue code for observer's pocket watch, 1939-1945.
6A/1072 Mk.IIB	Mark IIB eight-day aircraft clock with Royal Air Force issue code, c.1943.
6bb -	Royal Air Force prefix to NATO issue wristwatch.

GERMANY

RM 4102	Deutsche Reichsmarine issue watch mark, first used by the German Navy in 1848 although the RM title was not officially accepted until 1871. The mark continued in use until 1933.
[crown] M 1031	Traditional German Navy issue watch mark, 1871-1918.
[eagle] M	German Navy watch mark, c.1932.
K.M.	Kriegsmarine property mark, 1933-1945.

M 8621
I. KL
Kriegsmarine second class chronometer watch mark with naval issue number.

M13176
205725
Kriegsmarine issue watch mark with naval number and manufacturer's code number.

Kriegsmarine issue chronograph watch mark.

M
Artl. 5551
Kriegsmarine issue watch mark with Naval Artillery code.

9241
N
M
Marks on Kriegsmarine issue U-boat clock, coded for service with the North Sea fleet.

Kriegsmarine
Kriegsmarine issue clock mark.

D. 93512 H.
Deutsches Heer - German Army property mark with serial number, found only found on Swiss-made watches, 1939-1940.

D.I. . . . . H.
Deutsches Heer property mark found on non-waterproof wristwatches with sweeping centre seconds used for surveillance purposes, c.1943.

EIGENTUM
DER FLIEGERTRUPPEN
"Property of the Flying Corps" mark found on watches between 1914 and 1918.

F. Z.
L.
German Flying Corps mark found on pocket watches, pre-1918, with Zeppelin airship code.

P.u. W.
Geramn Flying Corps mark, pre-1918.

FL.22883
Mark on Luftwaffe watch with Flieger number, 1939-45. The first two digits (22) of the code identify an observer's watch.

Fl.23883
As above; a navigator's watch is identified by the first two digits (23) of the code.

Fl.25883
As above; a pilot's watch is identified by the first two digits (25) of the code.

Werk: A.Lange & Söhne
Nr. 213807
Fertiggestellt
Andreas Huber
München - Berlin
Typical manufacturer's and maker's details, 1933-1945.

RLM
NAV B - UHR
Reichs Luftfahrt Ministerium, Navigation Beobachtung Uhr - Reich Air Ministry issue navigation/ observation watch, 1933-1945.

D601214
Dienst number - service number found on standard Swiss-made Luftwaffe wristwatches, 1939-1945.

BUND
6645 - 12 - 194
Bundeswehr issue pilot's wristwatch with NATO stores code.

UNITED STATES OF AMERICA

U.S. MARITIME COMMISSION
United States Shipping Board merchant navy property watch mark, 1914-1940.

Official title of the US Shipping Board; mark found on watch dials from 1940.

U.S. NAVY
No. 9687
US Navy issue watch mark and serial number, c.1920.

BUREAU OF SHIPS
U.S. NAVY
Bureau of Ships property mark, used on US Navy issue watches since 1920.

U.S. NAVY
BU. SHIPS
US Navy Bureau of Ships, abbreviated form of above mark.

364 - 1941
US Naval Observatory mark bearing 1941 date, found on inspected chronometer watches.

NAVIGATION MASTERWATCH
US Navy issue high grade deck watch.

MTD.
CHRONOMETER WATCH
Mounted Chronometer Watch mark found on US Navy issue gimballed chronometer.

COMPARING WATCH
US Navy issue high grade watch with hacking device.

U.S.M.C.
United States Marine Corps issue watch.

U.S.C.G. No. 57	US Coast Guard mark on issue watch.	

CORPS OF ENGINEERS U.S.A. No. 1165	Corps of Engineers issue mark on chronograph watch, c.1917.
SIGNAL CORPS U.S.A.	Signal Corps issue watch mark, c.1917.
U.S. ARMY	US Army contract mark on Hamilton Mod.22 chronometer, c.1942.
(**U.S. ARMY**)	US Army property mark applied over US Navy issue stamps. The original markings have been milled away prior to reissue of the Hamilton Mod.22 to a different branch of the armed forces, probably post-1945.
U.S. GOVT.	US Government property mark found on the movement of high grade issue watches, 1939-1945.
A.N. 5740	Mark found on Army/Navy issue high grade pocket watches, including those issued to the Army Air Forces pre-1945.
ORD. DEPT. U.S.A.	US Army Ordnance Department issue watch, pre-1945.
ORD CORPS USA	US Army Ordnance Corps issue watch, post-1945.

US Ordnance Department codes used after 12 November 1940 to identify watch grades:

OA	7-9 jewel pocket watch.
OB	15-17 jewel pocket watch.
OC	7-9 jewel wristwatch.
OD	15-17 jewel wristwatch.
OE	21-jewel railroad grade pocket watch.
OF	15-17 jewel wristwatch with waterproof case.
OFA	15-16 jewel wristwatch in waterproof case; used as a Type A-11 substitute by the Army Air Corps/Air Forces (whose designation changed after June 1941).
OG	7-9 jewel wristwatch with waterproof case.
OS	Stop watch.

In the event of any overhaul, uncoded watches made prior to 12 November 1940 were marked at the time of repair with the following codes:

OW	7-9 jewel pocket watch.
OX	15-17 jewel pocket watch.
OY	7-9 jewel wristwatch.
OZ	15-17 jewel wristwatch.
BU. AERO U.S. NAVY	Issue watch mark, Bureau of Aeronautics (under the auspices of the US Navy), 1921-1959.
BU. AERO SER No.196 - 32	Bureau of Aeronautics issue watch bearing serial number and 1932 date.
U.S. ARMY A.C.	US Army Air Corps issue watch mark, 1926-1941.
AVIGATION WATCH	Abbreviated mark for "Aviation Navigation Watch", also designated as Type A-4, c.1934.
AIRCRAFT NAVIGATIONAL CHRONOGRAPH WATCH	US Army Air Corps pilot's/navigator's issue hacking watch designated as Type A-7, 1934-1940.
TYPE A - 1	The first watch to be standardised for US Army Air Corps use in 1926, designed for use in conjunction with the ground speed drift indicator.
TYPE A - 2	Master timepiece adopted in 1932, consisting of two watches housed in a wooden box, one calibrated to indicate solar time, the other sidereal time.
TYPE A - 3	Longines Wittnauer Weems patent watch adopted in 1932.
TYPE A - 4	Waltham "Avigation Watch" adopted in 1934, consisting of two pocket watches as in Type A-2.
TYPE A - 5	George H.Adamson-designed watch with a Waltham movement, incorporating a 24 hour dial. Tested in 1934 but not adopted for service until 1937.
TYPE A - 6	Similar watch to Type A-4, procured in limited numbers in 1934.

TYPE A - 7	"Aircraft Navigational Chronograph Watch" adopted in 1934, made from a pocket chronograph watch converted for use as a wristwatch.
TYPE A - 8	Pocket stop watch with ten second dial used for timing ground speed.
TYPE A - 9	Reworked Type A-5, adopted in 1940.
TYPE A - 10	This watch never passed the experimental stage.
TYPE A - 11	The standard US Air Corps/Air Forces wristwatch adopted in 1940, and manufactured in large numbers by several companies, 1940-1945.
TYPE A - 12	Elgin-made hacking wristwatch with 24 hour dial, adopted in 1940 but only issued in small numbers.
TYPE A - 13	Similar to the Type A-9, this master watch adopted in 1941 also features a hacking function.
TYPE A - 14	Never issued.
TYPE A - 15	Tested but never adopted.
TYPE A - 16	Similar to the Type A-11 but improved to be more tolerant of temperature changes; adopted in 1945 for US Army Air Forces use.
TYPE A - 17	Improved version of Type A-16, issued c.1950.
MILITARY TYPE III CLASS A	US Air Force digital quartz wristwatch, c.1980.

FRANCE

DEPÔT DE LA MARINE	French Navy stores mark, c.1910.
⚓ **MONTRE TORPILLEUR**	Torpedo Watch marking used on a French Navy chronometer watch, c.1900-1918.
SERVICE HYDROGRAPHIQUE DE LA MARINE	Hydrographic Service chronometer watch of the French Navy, c.1920-1940.
MARINE SERVICE HYDROGRAPHIQUE	French Navy issue chronometer watch.

MARINE NATIONALE	French Navy issue watch mark, post-1950.
MARINE NATIONALE AERONAUTIQUE NAVALE	French Navy issue pilot's watch, c.1950.
M G	Ministere de la Guerre - War Ministry property mark, 1914-1918 and c.1939
MINISTÈRE DE LA GUERRE • 163 • ARTILLERIE	War Ministry property mark for the Artillery.
MINISTÉRE DE L' AVIATION	French Air Ministry mark found on aircraft clocks, c.1915.
✰✰✰✰ ✰✰✰	Mark applied to dial of Hanhaldt chronograph wristwatch by the Dodane watch company, to obliterate German provenance, prior to reissue to the French Air Force post-1945.
TYPE 20	French Air Force issue pilot's chronograph wristwatch issued from 1954.
TYPE 21	French Air Force issue pilot's chronograph wristwatch issued in the 1960s.
C E V	Centre d'Essai en Vol - French Air Force test flight centre issue chronograph wristwatch.
FG 15 11 65	Fin de Garantie - quality control assurance mark followed by the inspection date, 15 November 1965.

CANADA

C. H. S. ↑ 1	Canadian Hydrographic Service code for naval issue gimballed chronometer watch, 1939-1946.
C. H. S. ↑ 2 **C. H. S. ↑ 3** **C. H. S. ↑ 4**	Royal Canadian Navy codes are the same as the Royal Navy issue markings with the addition of a "C" prefix.
C↑	Canadian military issue watch mark, 1939-1945.
R.C.A.F. REF. No. 6B/159 4368/42	Royal Canadian Air Force issue pilot's wristwatch, dated 1942.

CZECHOSLOVAKIA

MAJETEK VOJENSKÉ SPRÁVY 2922 — Property of Military Affairs - marking and issue number found on Czechoslovakian military watches, pre-1939.

For Air Force Use - marking found on some Czechoslovakian Air Force watches, c.1939.

ITALY

INSTITUTO IDROGRAPHICO R. MARINA — Hydrographic Institute - Royal Italian Navy issue watch mark used in the 1930s.

MARINA MILITARE — Italian Navy issue wristwatch mark.

R. AERONAUTICA — Regia Aeronautica - Royal Italian Air Force pilot's chronograph watch, pre-1945.

REPUBLIC OF CHINA

Chinese Navy issue wristwatch mark.

CHILE

MARINA DE CHILE — Chilean Navy issue chronometer watch.

SPAIN

NAVEGACION — Spanish merchant navy issue deck watch.

SWEDEN

702 — Swedish Navy issue chronometer watch.

JAPAN

Imperial Navy issue watch mark, pre-1945.

Japanese character mark on rear of Imperial Navy issue wristwatch, pre-1945.

Imperial Army issue watch mark, pre-1945.

AUSTRIA-HUNGARY

K. u. K. Kriegs Marine — Kaiserlich und Koeniglich Kriegs Marine - Imperial and Royal Navy issue chronometer watch, pre-1918.

POLAND

W P — Wojsko Polskie - Polish army property mark, pre-1939.

6B/159 A12696 P.A.F. — Polish Air Force issue mark found on Royal Air Force coded wristwatch, c.1940.

PERU

Peruvian Air Force property mark on a pilot's issue Rolex Cosmograph wristwatch, c.1975.

NETHERLANDS

Royal Dutch Army issue watch mark, c.1939.

USING THE PRICE GUIDE

Each entry in this book includes a guide to current price, and these have been compiled by reference to a number of sources. In the main, the information has been taken from auction house estimates and hammer prices. These prices are normally a good indication as to current market values; but as with all auction prices, they may sometimes reach exaggerated levels when two or more collectors bid against each other for a particularly rare or desirable timepiece. It is frequently the case that when such achieved prices become known, more examples of these "rare" timepieces will materialise, and in consequence their market value will then drop. Where auction values have not been available to the author, dealers' selling prices have been used as an alternative. Naturally these will also be subject to vagaries, as the dealer will have included his "mark-up".

The valuations are also based on the assumption that (unless otherwise stated) the timepiece is in, at least, good condition. The interpretation of "good condition" is naturally a somewhat subjective matter, and the vendor will tend to grade the piece rather more generously than the buyer. For the purposes of this guide, "good condition" will require the timepiece to be free from any significant mechanical defect, although it should be accepted that the watch may require routine servicing and cleaning; there should be no excessive wear or serious damage to the case or dial, which should be original. Inevitably, however, replacement parts may be encountered, in particular the winding crown. Provided that any replacement part does not detract from the character of the watch, it may be deemed acceptable. Clearly, then, examples of timepieces in poor or in mint condition may be worth far less or a great deal more than the median values quoted here. In some relevant entries the reader will find comparisons of the estimated values of pieces of the same model but produced by different manufacturers; this, too, can affect prices significantly. Pieces with any interesting attributed provenance may also fetch much higher prices even if in less than impressive condition; it is one of the attractions of collecting in any field of militaria that technically orthodox pieces may have dramatic historical associations which make them unusually desirable.

At the end of the day it is the individual collector who, having decided upon his or her own criteria, will have to choose what price is worth paying for any particular timepiece. It is hoped that these estimates will be of assistance in making that choice; but remember, they should only be seen as a guide.

DECK WATCHES & POCKET WATCHES

In the ferment of scientific and techological progress which followed the Industrial Revolution, every power of world stature sought to equip its armed forces with the fruits of the latest advances; and by the late years of the 19th century they enjoyed hitherto unimaginable opportunities to do so. This determination to obtain the best applied not only to battleships and machine guns; the leading nations did not hesitate to purchase quality examples of the most modern of military timepieces. Initially procurement agencies would look to their home manufacturing industry to meet their demands - as with this Imperial Russian Navy issue deck watch, circa 1885. Supplied by and signed "J. WIREN, St. PETERSBURG," this watch epitomises the quality that was available for selective issue. It has an "up and down" dial calibrated from 0 to 30 hours, just below the 12 o'clock position; as the main spring winds down, the running time of the watch is automatically displayed. This useful feature prevents the unnecessary handling of the watch, which has to be wound with a key. To further secure it the watch is kept in a fitted mahogany box, which is emblazoned with the Russian double-headed eagle. (Courtesy Sotheby's)

Value *£750-£850*

At the turn of the century the British Admiralty conducted an entire series of trials to determine the suitability of watches for issue to the Royal Navy as marine timekeepers. To this end the Naval Observatory was inundated with watches for evaluation. As and when they were judged worthy, watch companies such as Kendal & Dent of London earned the right to advertise their achievement. Predominantly this was done in the most conspicuous manner by writing "MAKERS TO THE ADMIRALTY" across the dials and on the movements of their watches. This example, which retains its original box, dates from circa 1910. It has a silver case and a movement of 17 jewel lever type, and has been fitted with a micrometer balance adjustment.

Value £75-£85

Delicate mechanical watch movements are prone to damage from the effects of shock, or the ingress of dirt and water - which are conditions that the military timepiece frequently has to endure. To overcome these problems at least to some degree, certain watchmakers protected their movements by employing robust, close-fitting cases which screwed together to form at least some barrier to the elements. A thick bevelled crystal glass would also be used to give the dial added protection. This example was made and supplied to the British Army by W. Eberhardt of London, circa 1900. The movement was of their own unusual design, the balance wheel mechanism being mounted onto the top plate while the majority of the other moving parts were covered. This may have provided some slight protection to the internal components of the movement, but it made any subsequent repair of the watch unnecessarily awkward. Note also the broad arrow mark which is repeated on the movement and case. (Courtesy D.Penny)

Value *£60-£70*

This military pocket watch is complete with its original leather presentation case, which bears the name "J.W Benson Ltd. Watchmakers, Jewellers & Silversmiths, 62 & 64 LUDGATE HILL E.C.4." The inside cuvette of the watch is engraved "By Warrant to H.M. The Late Queen Victoria", which inscription dates the watch conveniently to 1901. The 15 jewel movement is unsigned, although the calibre number 19.75 is marked on it; this number does in fact identify the maker as Longines.

Unusual as it may seem, this is a common practice watchmakers frequently remain anonymous. Even houses of high standing, such as Longines, supplied watches to others and allowed the third party to put their own name to the watch. On the rear of the nickel case is the British broad arrow emblem over "I", indicating issue in India.

Value *£100-£120*

"THE BISLEY WATCH", as the dial legend reads, is a commemorative watch made circa 1905. It celebrates the famous Bisley Camp shooting grounds at Brookwood, Surrey, built by the National Rifle Association in 1890. Retailed by H.Steward of London, this watch would have been deliberately aimed to appeal to the many military and civilian target shooters who attended Bisley.
Value *£40-£50*

By the time this pocket watch was procured, circa
1910, the Longines name had already gained
prominence. Longines were by now the recipients
of numerous awards for timekeeping excellence, so
it is not surprising that the military, even in times
of relative peace, should seek to buy their products.
This issue timepiece shows signs of the latest
design innovations which assist in the hand-setting
routine. The earlier "pin set" device had now been
replaced by a more modern system, whereby the
hands could be set by first pulling the winder out
one stop. This simple but effective feature meant
that the time could be set more rapidly, even with
gloved hands. The case back bears a crudely
applied broad arrow mark.
Value *£60-£70*

The Royal Artillery was among the first British military organisations to be issued with general service watches, from around 1885. Presumably it must have been considered a priority to provide artillery officers with the means to ensure that their bombardments would occur at a predetermined time and for exact periods. The earliest examples of these timepieces encountered are no more than good standard commercial grade pocket watches, with either English or Swiss movements. This example of a Royal Artillery issue pocket watch of circa 1915 has an engraved contract number and "RA" property mark. Behind the screw back is a fine quality adjusted Swiss movement of unknown origin, which is jewelled to the centre employing screwed chatons. A further refinement is the use of a micrometer regulator on the balance cock. Although the glass has become scratched over the years, giving the dial a faded appearance in this picture, note the very large, high visibility luminous numerals.

Value *£50-£60*

H. Williamson Ltd. of London manufactured a variety of 7 jewel pocket watches for the British armed forces, circa 1914. Some of their earlier contract watches utilised movements from the company's stock which, if it were not for the exigencies of war, would have been destined for use in one of their hunting case watches. Consequently these issue timepieces have the subsidiary seconds dial at the 3 o'clock position. Other examples can be found with the more traditional form of dial layout, in both black luminescent and white enamel dials. Each one of these watches is in a Dennison-made case and heavily marked with a serial number which is repeated on the dial, case side and screw back, together with the broad arrow. Williamson also produced a number of higher jewelled eight-day pocket watches, some of which were procured for issue to the Royal Flying Corps. **Value** *£40-£50*

This French pocket watch, of unknown make, circa
1914 portrays on the back of the case the
embossed likeness of General Joffre and the legend
"J.J.C.JOFFRE GENERALISSIME DES
ARMEES FRANCAISES 1914", (a clearer image
of the same design will be found on page 58). This
imagery typifies the naive patriotism of the
European nations at the start of the First World
War. By 1918 the horrors of modern warfare were
all too well understood; and watches produced for
the French market by Omega in 1918 bore images
representing the Angel of Peace.
Value *£80-£90*

Although this watch does not bear any military property stamps, it does have certain attributes which
would make it an admirable service timepiece. The
retailer, Birch & Gaydon Ltd. of London, supplied
the British military with equipment throughout the
Great War and, as is probably the case with this
watch, also retailed their stock privately to members
of the armed forces. The watch itself was made by
the Swiss maker Zenith, circa 1915, employing an
unusual 15 jewel movement with a built-in alarm
which is operated by a second spring barrel and a
hammer which strikes against a gong. Clever case
design also enabled the user to position the watch
upright on an integral stand.
Value *£150-£175*

THE SMITH
8-DAY AVIATION WATCH

Type No. AA 684—non-luminous.
„ **AA 685**—luminous.

Because of its splendid time-keeping and unfailing accuracy this instrument has gained the reputation of being the most successful watch yet designed for constant use on Aircraft. Thousands were supplied to the British Government during the war, and with the most satisfactory results. A fully jewelled and compensated lever movement is used in this model, resulting in a watch of extreme reliability, combined with the highest class workmanship and finish. It is fitted in a special mounting for screwing to the instrument board, and can be supplied with either black or white dials, and luminous or non-luminous as desired.

For Prices see pages at the end of this section.

On 13 April 1912 the British Army's Royal Flying Corps was created, replacing the short-lived Air Battalion of the Royal Engineers. The RFC was to train aviators at a Central Flying School, and to develop both a military and a naval wing within its own ranks; these wings, while under the auspices of the RFC, were administered separately by the War Department and the Admiralty. On the eve of the First World War in 1914 the naval wing, keen to develop according to the special flying needs of the fleet, severed its connection with the RFC, and the Royal Naval Air Service was born.

The timepieces issued to the RFC and the RNAS are ostensibly the same, although the naval watches would appear to be predominantly of eight-day pattern. Bows were not fitted to the long shank around the winding stem, as the timepiece was not intended for wearing by the aviator; the watch was to be placed into a special holder mounted on the aircraft's instrument panel, as seen in the "Aviation Watch" advertisement.

As the Admiralty Department mark on the dial
suggests, this watch is an early and rare aviator's
Mark II timepiece from the naval wing of the
RFC, circa 1913. An unusually long "broad arrow"
emblem, running vertically the length of the snap-
back case, also adorns this example. The movement, retailed by Thomas Armstrong & Bro. of
Manchester, was made by the Octavia Watch Co.
of Switzerland and is of eight-day pattern. These
particular movements were also used during the
First World War for many of the RFC's Mark IV
aviation watches.

Value *£130-£150*

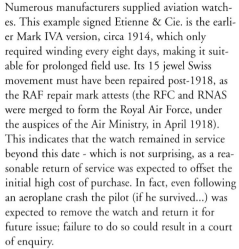

Numerous manufacturers supplied aviation watches. This example signed Etienne & Cie. is the earlier Mark IVA version, circa 1914, which only required winding every eight days, making it suitable for prolonged field use. Its 15 jewel Swiss movement must have been repaired post-1918, as the RAF repair mark attests (the RFC and RNAS were merged to form the Royal Air Force, under the auspices of the Air Ministry, in April 1918). This indicates that the watch remained in service beyond this date - which is not surprising, as a reasonable return of service was expected to offset the initial high cost of purchase. In fact, even following an aeroplane crash the pilot (if he survived...) was expected to remove the watch and return it for future issue; failure to do so could result in a court of enquiry.

Value *£80-£100*

The Mark V aviator's watch, circa 1916, was made available from a variety of manufacturers including Electa, Doxa, Omega and Zenith; other makers remain anonymous, having left their movements unsigned. Every watch had a 15 jewel movement, selected for its ability to maintain accurate time despite constant vibration while fitted to the aeroplane's instrument panel. Basically the Mark V was available in three types, the standard 30-hour non-luminous pattern being preferred. Later a luminous version was also used by night fighters.

However, the constant vibration caused the radium paint to disintegrate; the particles of paint would penetrate the delicate movement, leading to malfunctions. The third type is the eight-day variant, which was still demanded in certain quarters. The bow seen in the photograph has been added at a later date.
Value *£50-£60 (Electa), £50-£60 (Doxa), £80-£100 (Omega), £90-£100 (Zenith)*

There can be no argument as to the ownership of
this watch, as the dial is clearly marked "EIGEN-
TUM DER FLIEGERTRUPPEN". This type of
watch, with its inverted dial, was worn suspended
from a fob on the German aviator's flying suit - a
practical means of rapid access, especially at high
altitude when bulky garments would make it difficult to check any conventional watch quickly.
The rear of this gunmetal case is stamped with
the Flying Corps' winged propeller insignia and
FLZ; these abbreviations indicate that it was used
by a member of a Zeppelin airship crew, circa
1915. During that year London suffered its first
ever air raid, when Zeppelin LZ38 reached the
north-east of the capital on 31 May. By 1918 a
total of 115 Zeppelins had been built; this suggests that not many watches could have been
issued in total, making this timepiece a rarity.
Inside the case there is an unsigned Swiss 15 jewel
movement which was supplied to the German
Flying Corps by Schoetensack & Nusch of Berlin.
(Courtesy R.Rose)
Value *£200-£250*

The Zeppelin raids obliged the RFC to mount a night air defence effort, and fighter squadrons were based at airfields around London and trained in this extremely hazardous new discipline. In the Great War all aircraft handling and most navigation was performed very much "by eye", with minimal help from instruments. With enough runway and no awkward church towers or trees at the end, taking off was straightforward enough; but locating a flying target in the dark was virtually impossible unless it chanced to be pinpointed by nearby searchlights; there was a risk of mid-air collision if several fighters hunted the same patch of sky; and most importantly, the pilot would sooner rather than later face the need to find his way back to his airfield and make a landing, guided only by rudimentary ground flares. It is hardly surprising that it was September 1916 before the first air-to-air night airship kill was claimed.

Night flying naturally required a close check to be kept on the elapsed time and fuel; and for that reason a number of Mark V Luminous pocket watches were ordered. This example made by Omega, circa 1917, has skeleton hands which have lost the majority of the radium paint - possibly as a result of the same impact which damaged the dial. Bold luminous dots alongside the numerals would have made the watch easily legible at night.
Value £50-£60 *(damaged)*

When the Royal Air Force was formed from the
RFC and RNAS in April 1918 the timepieces used
by the Royal Flying Corps remained in service
under the newly established Air Ministry. This
early eight-day Mark IVA aviator's pocket watch,
circa 1914, is unusual in having the dial marked
with the broad arrow "Aviation" emblem. More
interesting still is the addition of the King's Crown
AM mark to the hack of the case, to eliminate the
former WD property mark.
Value *£80-£100*

During 1915, while the United States was not yet a combatant, America did offer assistance to the British government by supplying arms together with other items of military equipment, including watches. These field pocket watches manufactured by the Elgin National Watch Co. had a nickel screw-back case engraved with the broad arrow and service number. These watches, which employed Elgin 16 size, 7 or 17 jewel movements, went on to become one of the company's primary models. In the early 1940s the British armed forces were once again receiving Elgin's field pocket watches, produced with only minor but significant modifications from the original.

Value *£50-£60*

When the first operational tanks arrived on the battlefield of the Somme on 15 September 1916 to support the attack of the British Fourth Army, their crews shared a single steel cabin with a massive, unshielded Daimler engine, two side-mounted 6-pounder naval guns, and four machine guns. Apart from the deafening noise, exhausting heat and sickening fumes, the violent movement kept the crews in constant danger of serious injury from being thrown against the internal machinery and fixtures. Any timepiece used under such conditions had a very limited life expectancy indeed; and rather than continuously replace damaged standard issue timepieces, the Army issued tank crews with these inexpensive Ingersoll pocket watches. Basic in the extreme, they proved adequate timekeepers for the short life that was expected of them. Each watch had a heavily luminised radium dial for reading in the dark, smoke-filled interior of the tank. The back of the case may be found marked with the broad arrow above "TW" for Tank Watch.
Value *£20-£25*

Not only were the French company of Leroy & Cie. credited with being watchmakers to the French Navy, but they were also responsible for supplying chronometer watches to the Royal Navy. This fine example of a deck watch was issued to the RN in about 1920. The silver case is engraved on the snap back "H.S.2", together with the broad arrow property mark, which is repeated on the 17 jewel movement and again on the dial. (Courtesy Kent Sales)
Value *£400-£500*

Vacheron & Constantin of Geneva produced a number of first class Beobachtungsuhren (observation watches) for the Kriegsmarine, circa 1938. This particular B-uhr uses the 21 jewel calibre 162 movement, which is equipped with a state-of-wind register just below the 12 o'clock position. Another B-uhr variant employed a 19 jewel Chronometer Royal movement, which only features a subsidiary seconds dial. Engraved on the reverse of the heavy duty silver case is the Kriegsmarine eagle over "M" property marking. These timepieces were

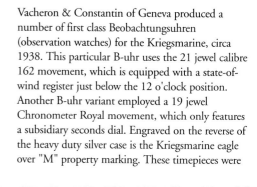

carried on a number of classes of vessel engaged on protracted sea voyages; typically, U-boats and destroyers would carry one first class B-uhr among their complement of navigational equipment, while cruisers and battleships would carry three such timepieces. Vacheron & Constantin also supplied Chronometer Royal and 21 jewel calibre 163 watches (similar to calibre 162 but again without the auxiliary state-of-wind register) to the Royal Navy; these can be identified by the broad arrow and "H.S.2" markings. (Courtesy Kent Sales)
Value *£1,000-£1,200*

In 1943 the Kriegsmarine approached the
International Watch Company of Schaffhausen to
supply a quantity of second class rated deck
watches. In the event only about 300 of these were
obtained from IWC, and each one was allocated to
a U-boat. The white enamel dial is fully signed by
the manufacturer and marked with the KM
property stamp; the rear of the screw-back
nickel case is stamped with the Kriegsmarine eagle
and swastika over an M-prefixed issue number. The
addition of the II.Kl. marking classified the official

Value *£500-£600*

rating of the 17 jewel movement. Meanwhile,
most other second class deck watches were being
used on board fast coastal craft such as E-boats and
R-boats in preference to the more expensive eight-
day chronometers; typically such vessels left port
for brief patrols only, and navigators could
frequently adjust their deck watches in port against
a master time source. Despite their second class
rating these watches performed admirably as they
had to: given the high speed of the craft on which
they were habitually used, calculation of distance
travelled relied upon a close check of elapsed time.

Lange & Sohne are Germany's most celebrated
watchmakers, and they produced some of the
finest deck watches for the Kriegsmarine. For this
first class naval observation watch, circa 1943,
Lange have used their 16 jewel calibre 48 movement, which has a swan neck regulator on the balance. A 35-hour state-of-wind indicator and a subsidiary seconds dial can be seen on the silvered
watch face. To complement the appearance of the
dial blued steel hands have been used. These are
set by first depressing the pin set device, which is
situated just above the 1 o'clock position. After
1945 many of these watches where retained by the
French, who removed all trace of the Nazi
emblems before they were reissued to the French
Navy. (Courtesy Kent Sales)
Value *£700-£800*

The British armed forces were slow to embrace change, and consequently, when war loomed once more in 1939, the War Department was caught ill-prepared. Pocket watches were hurriedly purchased by the procurement office from numerous Swiss makers and from commercial retailers, in anticipation of the shortages that were likely to follow. Most of these pocket watches were regarded as "General Service" timepieces and classified as "Temporary Pattern". While more appropriate watches were not yet available to the Army in sufficient numbers these "GSTP" pocket watches had to suffice, becoming the workhorses of the Army's horological instruments. "General Service" watches were exactly that. They fulfilled the role of the contemporary timekeeper for routine duties such as those performed, for example, by radio operators and drivers. Each Swiss-produced GSTP watch had a 15 jewel movement, luminous black or white dial and subsidiary seconds dial. Cases were normally provided with snap backs, although some do have screw backs. This particular Leonidas pocket watch is a typical example of the standard British Army GSTP.
Value £25-£30

Pocket watches were available to the German Army only in limited numbers. They had nickel cases with screw backs which required a special three-pin spanner to open them; this not only ensured that the case was tightly secured against damp and dirt, but prevented inquisitive prying into the movement by clumsy soldiers. Behind the back a secondary dust cover would be fitted over the movement. 15 jewel movements were used as standard; no shock protection was fitted, however, as the authorities considered this an extravagant expense on a watch that was normally to be carried safely in an officer's pocket (an odd view of the realities of 20th century warfare). This example was produced by Zenith, circa 1939; others were supplied by Arsa.
Value *£70-£80 (Zenith), £40-£50 (Arsa)*

Military Rolex pocket watches were available, circa 1939, in two styles, with either a black luminous or a white non-luminous dial. The black dial pocket watch was evaluated by the British Army and given the grade "General Service Mark II". The white dial version was not intended for pocket use, and was constructed in a case without a chain bow. This was so that the watch could be inserted in a receptacle within a protective wooden case, or on a vehicle instrument panel. The second pattern was designated by the Army as a "B" type, or "back-up" timepiece to a chronometer watch. The "B" mark used to prefix the issue number of the watch was stamped on the rear of the screw back and on the side of the casing. The GS Mk.II watch had all the issue numbers prefixed with the letter "A". The movements of both models are signed by Rolex on the dial case and movement, which is also marked "15 Rubies". These Rolex movements are actually manufactured as ebauches by the Cortebert watch company, based on Cortebert's calibre 526 movement.

Value *£250-£350*

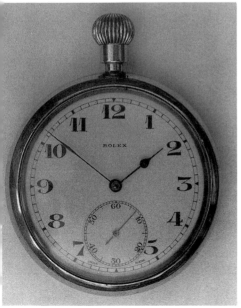

This Cortebert "Extra" pocket watch, designated as a General Service Timepiece, is housed in a soft alloy screw-back case; this example is marked on the back with the broad arrow, "G.S.T.P"., and "T7905". Made by Cortebert circa 1942, the signed calibre 526 movement is also marked "15 Rubies". This movement bears a striking resemblance to the Rolex military pocket watch movement - unsurprisingly, as Cortebert supplied ebauches to Rolex based on the calibre 526 movement. Although superficially the connecting bridge work follows a different layout, all the working parts are interchangeable between the two models.
Value *£30-£40*

This 15 jewel British Army issue General Service Timepiece, circa 1939, has survived in pristine condition, with the white enamel dial retaining all its original luminous paint. This scarce example was supplied by the renowned maker Omega, whose name and trademark appear on the dial. Omega were first contracted by the British during the First World War, when they supplied motor vehicle clocks for Army trucks. However, between 1939 and 1945 the British were supplied with huge quantities of Omega watches which totalled over 100,000 pieces. These represented over half the total number of timepieces procured by the British armed forces during the war. After the Allied victory Field Marshal Montgomery visited the Biel factory and personally thanked the staff at Omega for their work towards the war effort. **Value** *£70-£80*

Special rubber coverings were made to fit over
pocket watches which might be subjected to harsh
conditions. This example has been fitted to a
Helvetia GSTP which already shows signs of damage to the dial. Note also that the hour hand is a
contemporary replacement which does not make
the correct pair to the minute hand.
Value *£15-£20*

Royal Air Force issue pocket watches differ from the Army's GSTPs only in being non-luminous. 15 jewel pocket watches were often chosen by navigators in preference to wristwatches, especially during night bombing operations. The navigators found it useful to place their pocket watches on the charts from which they were working, and the watch's size meant that the time could be read more easily. On this fine Jaeger Le Coultre watch note the size of the subsidiary seconds dial; much larger than the configuration on a normal watch dial, it emphasises the importance of elapsing seconds in certain operational circumstances. The back of this case is marked "6E/50", "A1027C" below the broad arrow.

Value *£60-£80*

Early during the Second World War the Hamilton Watch Company of America began work on their latest chronometer watch. In 1942 the new Model 22, with its 21 jewel movement which was adjusted to temperature and six positions, became available in two versions. A "mounted" (gimballed) chronometer watch was housed within a three-tier wooden case. Alternatively, the "non-gimbal" type was furnished in a large, conventional style pocket watch case and kept within a padded wooden box. These chronometers had a 48-hour power reserve which was indicated on the dial. The hands are set by first depressing the pin to the left of the winder. Most of the Model 22s were used by the US Navy for navigational purposes; these are engraved on the case back and movement "BUREAU OF SHIPS U.S. NAVY". Some of the non-gimbal variety saw service in Patrol Torpedo boats. By 1948 most of the non-gimbal watches were given over to the US Army Transportation Corps. (Courtesy Sotheby's)
Value *£800-£1,000 (gimballed), £550-£650 (non-gimbal)*

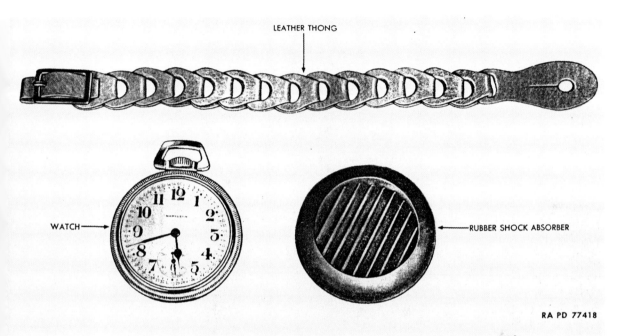

LEATHER THONG

WATCH →

← RUBBER SHOCK ABSORBER

RA PD 77418

Figure 47 – Watch With Rubber Shock Absorber and Leather Thong Removed

The following pages include extracts taken from a US technical manual (TM 9-1575) concerning the repair and maintenance of issue timepieces, dating from 6 April 1945 and entitled "Ordnance Maintenance Wristwatches, Pocket Watches, Stop Watches and Clocks". This is an ideal reference to the types of watches in use by the US forces during the Second World War.

Figure 47 illustrates the Hamilton 16 size, model 992B pocket watch. Developed in 1941, these 21 jewel railroad grade timepieces made use of Hamilton's specially developed hair spring, which was a remarkable metallurgical achievement, making it totally impervious to magnetism and corrosion. Further proof of Hamilton's attention to detail was the enamel dial, which had every second division individually numbered from 1 to 60. The watch case was of a three-part dustproof type, made of either nickel or chrome-plated base metal; the back was engraved with "U.S. ORDNANCE DEPT. WATCH R.R. GRADE", together with

various other specification details, and the serial number was prefixed with the code "OE". On some of the watches the branch of service was also engraved on the movement. During the war the US Army purchased a total of 18,938 watches at a cost of $38.96 each; most of these were issued to the Corps of Engineers.
Value *£150-£200*

In 1942 Hamilton began production of a chronometer quality "Navigation Master Watch". This watch, designated the Model 3992B, was originally made for the Royal Canadian Navy; it has a 22 jewel movement, and was only made up to 1945. During this time 2,494 timepieces were despatched to Canada. Others, like this example numbered 1290 and dated 1942, made their way to England where they saw service with the Royal Navy. Following the war many of these watches went into storage with the Chronometer Section of the Hydrographic Department, situated at Herstmonceux Castle near Hailsham, Sussex. This watch also bears an Air Ministry issue number which would have been added circa 1960, when these watches were pressed into service, primarily with RAF Vulcan bomber stations. From the paperwork that accompanies this watch it is apparent that it has been back to Herstmonceux for routine inspection and servicing. On 16 October 1980 this example was sent out to RAF St.Athan, where it completed its service life. The watch is complete with its original wooden transit case.

Value *£250-£280*

7-JEWEL

17-JEWEL

ORD. DEPT.
U.S.A.
No. OA-3820

ORD. DEPT.
U.S.A.
No. OC-3707

RA PD 78860

Figure 73 — Elgin Pocket Watches, 7- and 17-jewel, 16 Size —
Front and Back

As a pioneering company, Elgin were always looking for ways to improve the performance of their timepieces. Their endeavours led to the development of a very accurate hair spring made from an alloy which was called Elginium. The chief benefit of Elginium was its superior ability to withstand extremes in climatic temperature. Elginium was used in the manufacture of the two grades of field issue pocket watches shown in Figure 73 of TM 9-1575. The 7 jewel watch was referred to as Grade 291; the 17 jewel version, with damascened movement and balance micrometer regulator as standard, was catalogued as Grade 387. Both types came in a snap-back base metal case with a rope design decorating the outer edge, and luminous dials. The majority of these watches served with artillery units, but they also saw extensive use in airborne and transportation operations. The Grade 291 Elgin watch was exported to England, in a plain screw-back case and fitted with a black luminous dial, and was issued to the military as a General Service Timepiece.

Value *£40-£45 (Grade 291), £60 -£80 (Grade 387)*

Figure 93 in TM 9-1575 refers to the Waltham US Army issue 16 size field pocket watches.

Figure 93 — Waltham Pocket Watches, 9- and 17-jewel, 16 Size — Front and Back

Waltham produced two field grade US Army Ordnance pocket watches during the Second World War, the Model 1609 with 9 jewels and the Model 1617 with 17 jewels. Basically they were the same watch, employing the 16 size movement. Early examples, circa 1941, have white dials, and cost $12.50 for the Model 1609 and $24.63 for the Model 1617. By 1944, when the first batches of the Model 1609 arrived in England, a black luminous dial was also being used. These were primarily for issue to the Royal Navy, as with this example, which is marked on the back of the screw case with a small broad arrow. Unusually, however, some Waltham Model 1609 pocket watches were issued to the Army and,

despite having only a 9 jewel movement, they were given the status of "General Service Timepiece" in recognition of the accuracy and reliability of the movement, which was adjusted for temperature and three positions. After the war Waltham pocket watches continued to be purchased for the Royal Navy well into the 1950s, remaining in service into the 1960s. Post-1945 many of these watches were marked with the 0552 code, and the RN model can be identified by a small encircled "T" emblem. **Value** *£45-£50 (Model 1609), £50-£60 (Model 1617)*

In 1942 Zenith supplied the Royal Navy with a fine quality deck watch. These were fitted in "staybrite" screw-back cases engraved with the Hydrographic Service "H.S.3" code and broad arrow mark. The 15 jewel movement was equipped with a micrometer adjustable balance and centre seconds hand. The watch's issue number "7670", marked on the white enamel dial, is made up of the last four digits of the movement's serial number. These deck watches are based on the same movement that was used in the production of the Royal Flying Corps issue timepieces circa 1916. The earlier movements only differ in having subsidiary seconds dials.
Value *£120-£150*

After the war the Zenith HS3 deck watches went into storage at the Chronometer Section of the Hydrographic Department at Herstmonceaux Castle; there, during the 1950s, they had their enamel dials replaced with special decimal dials, using smaller hour and minute hands. This indicates that the watches' "time-telling" ability is of only secondary importance to their main intended function. The dial layout gives emphasis to minutes, which are picked out in red on the intermedi-

ate chapter ring; and an outer ring has been calibrated to indicate 100 units per minute. These watches were particularly useful for rapid mathematical calculations, where time equations could be more readily determined and expressed in terms of decimals. At the time of alteration the screw-back case has had the original "H.S.3" mark cancelled and has been engraved with new NATO stores numbers; "6183" is made up from the last four digits of the movement's serial number.
Value *£120-£150*

By modern standards pocket watches may be considered "old fashioned"; however, when it comes to practicality in applied use, there is still a place for them in the military. This example by CWC, dated 1977, is a non-luminous timepiece used by the Royal Navy; the screw back bears the "0552" issue code. The size of these watches, and the high contrast between numerals and dial, make them legible even in a poorly lit environment. These non-luminous watches have to be used on board nuclear

submarines in place of the luminous variety, since all luminous watches use a radioactive source to provide the dial with its irridescent quality. While the radiation emitted by a watch may be minimal, the on-board Geiger counters used as part of the submarine's safety system would eventually pick up an increase in generated atmospheric radiation, triggering alarms warning of a suspected leak from the nuclear generator. Consequently, the encircled "T" for Tritium mark, present on other watches of the same type, is absent from the dial of all submariners' watches.

Value *£20-£25*

WRISTLETS & WRISTWATCHES

Early wristwatches, which were widely available by 1914, were known as "wristlets", and were no more than small fob watches attached to a leather wrist band by the flimsiest of wire lugs. These wristlets were easily damaged due to their exposed position, which did not endear them to the British military authorities. The bureaucratic mind saw no advantage to their general issue, judging them as being of no more than ornamental value; and so the issue of robust pocket watches continued. However, many soldiers chose to purchase their own wristlet in preference, discovering through experience the benefits of having a rapidly accessible timekeeper. In fact, these notions were not new.

The Imperial German Navy had for some time been issuing its officers with wristlets manufactured by Girard Perigeaux, ever since a German naval engagement in the late 19th century when a naval artillery officer reported to his superiors that it was an unnecessary hindrance for him to be holding on to his pocket watch while timing and co-ordinating the artillery bombardment. He went on to report that to overcome the problem he had bound the pocket watch to his wrist. Later, in 1902, the Omega company was to bring out an advertisement which featured a British artillery officer wearing one of their wristlets, which it was claimed he had found to be "An indispensable item of military equipment."

This somewhat battered example, with its silver case hallmarked 1915, retailed by S.Smith & Son Ltd., Trafalgar Square, bears the presentation inscription "C.L.V.R. [City of London Volunteer Reserve] PRESENTED TO SERGT. L.R.PARK BY THE OFFICERS N.C.O.'s & MEN OF D COY TO REPLACE THE WATCH SMASHED BY A SHELL." This legend says it all. The vulnerability of such watches is also apparent through the amount of damage suffered by the case; remarkably, however, the watch still works.

Value £50- *(due to poor condition)*

Watch manufacturers quickly realised that wristlets which were to be used as active service timepieces required certain attributes. One of the first features to become standard for the majority of military timepieces was the use of luminous dials to assist in night operations when the use of a naked light would not be appropriate. Meanwhile other problems proved harder to overcome, such as how to protect the movement from water and dirt under front line conditions. One partially effective idea was

a closely fitting case which did away with an opening at the back; instead, the movement could only be accessed through the front of the wristlet. To do this the winder would first be disconnected to allow the bezel to be unscrewed complete with the movement. This design is commonly termed as a Borgel case after its designer. Advertisements for Borgel watches appeared in military publications in 1914.

The majority of wristlets produced had subsidiary seconds dials; these made the monitoring of elapsed seconds unnecessarily awkward, and so a centre second hand was developed for those who required precise short interval timing. It was especially suitable for medical personnel in pulse taking, for aviators in calculating the ground speed of their aircraft, and for any observation purposes where a stop watch was not available. This example has a Borgel case made of 9k. gold and is hallmarked 1915. These watches were retailed through Army & Navy Stores catalogues which were published for the British armed forces.
Value *£250-£300*

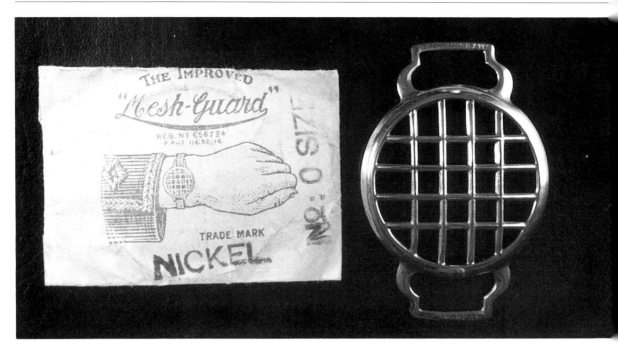

Protective covers were available in a variety of sizes and styles to fit virtually all wristlets. This example of "The Improved MeshGuard" is seen with its original paper wrapper depicting the wrist of an Army officer. The "MeshGuard" was a simple but effective way of protecting the watch glass against accidental damage.

Cyma, amongst other watch companies, took the idea of the "Mesh-Guard" one stage further by producing their wristlets with integral covers hinged at one end. The watch was well protected, yet still allowed the wearer a clear view. This pattern of wristlet is frequently referred to as a "trench watch." (Courtesy Sotheby's)
Value *£100-£120*

A variation on the theme of the "trench watch" is the hunting cased wristlet. While offering the highest level of protection to the glass, it does degrade the immediate visiblity of the dial. This watch would have appealed to any patriotic French soldier, as the cover - once again - portrays the likeness of General Joffre, the victor of the Marne in 1914 and supreme Allied commander 1914-16. This wristlet is made by an unknown Swiss company.
Value *£100-£120*

In the world of commerce retailers use a variety of means to make their products appeal to the purchaser. This silver wristlet sold by Mappin of London, circa 1915, has the title "CAMPAIGN" printed on the dial, which was certainly intended to stir warlike emotions. The 15 jewel movement is unsigned but the calibre number 13.34 identifies it as being made by Longines. While this wristlet may not be an Army issue timepiece it almost certainly would have belonged to an Army officer. Support for this supposition comes from the pro-

tective cover which has been fitted and the leather strap of military one-piece "safety" pattern. An identical watch is also shown without the cover. **Value** *£150-£175 (with protective cover)*

Probably as a result of popular demand, the War Department procured a variety of wristlets for evaluation and issue, circa 1917. All the wristlets that were made available have a number of different unsigned Swiss 15 jewel lever movements, while the case designs came in two types. Some had snap-back cases, which could not form an adequate hermetic seal and consequently were judged unsuitable for field conditions; many of these were sold off as surplus in the 1920s and bear the broad arrow cancellation mark. Other wristlets came with screw-back cases which offered better protection. All the wristlets had black enamel dials and radium numerals and hands.

Value *£90-£100 (snap-back), £100-£120 (screwback)*

hen the US Expeditionary Forces joined the First
orld War in 1917, elements of the Army Signal
orps were issued with wristlets procured from the
viss company Zenith. (It may be significant that
rly US military aviators were recruited from the
gnal Corps, which had its own flying wing.)
enith was a relatively new name in the market-
ace, which had first appeared on watches only in
011; but despite this Zenith had already won
umerous awards for excellence in the manufacture

of chronometer watches, a factor that would not
have been overlooked by the US War Department.
Each wristlet had a snap-back nickel case with
articulated lugs. The white enamel dial has radium-
coated numerals and hands, plus an inner set of
24-hour numerals in red. The words "SIGNAL
CORPS" have also been added to the dial - the
only property marks on these watches. The Zenith
name surmounts the subsidiary seconds dial. Inside
the case, the 15 jewel movement is an exact replica
in miniature of the company's existing pocket
watch movements; even the micrometer regulator
on the balance has been miniaturised.
Value *£450-£550*

In India the West End Watch Company supplied
the government with the majority of their timepieces from their outlet in Bombay. This wristlet,
circa 1925, has the name "SECUNDUS" on the
white dial; however, the 15 jewel Swiss movement
is unsigned. The plated snap-back case suggests
that the watch was not intended for field use; it is
probable that it was issued to the Police
Department. A thick crystal glass does offer the
dial some protection from knocks. The back of the
watch bears "SIS" and the broad arrow mark.
Rolex movements have been encountered in this
type of issue wristlet.
Value *£35-£45, £400-£450 (Rolex)*

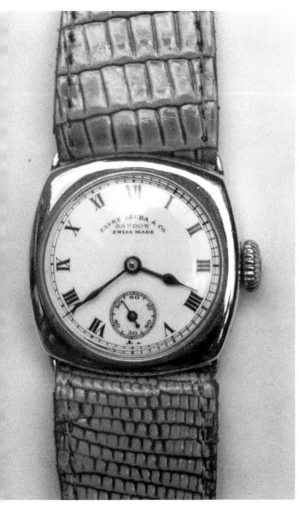 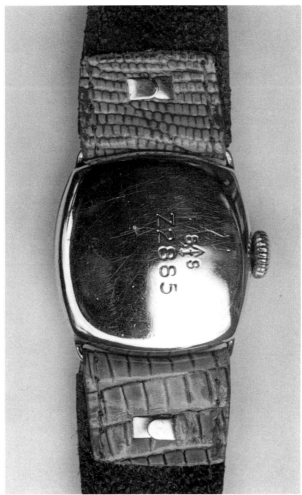

This rolled gold, cushion-shaped wristwatch was
issued to the British diplomatic corps in India.
Supplied by Favre Leuba & Co., circa 1935, it was
provided for official functions to those without a
suitable dress watch for the occasion. Certainly its
classically elegant appearance, with Roman numerals on the enamel dial, gave the watch a certain aes-
thetic appeal. The movement itself was of conventional 15 jewel form. The snap-on case back bears
the Indian broad arrow and watch issue number.
Value *£60-£70*

This commercially produced 15 jewel wristwatch of rectangular form, circa 1939, would not be worthy of comment if it were not for the crude engraving on the rear of its steel case, probably hastily applied by the owner in an attempt to avoid pilfering. It reads "1987641 D.H.WOOD, H.M.S.HOOD, 1940". In May 1941 Vice-Admiral Holland flew his flag on *HMS Hood* when he led the Battle Cruiser Squadron from Scapa Flow to intercept the battleships *Bismark* and

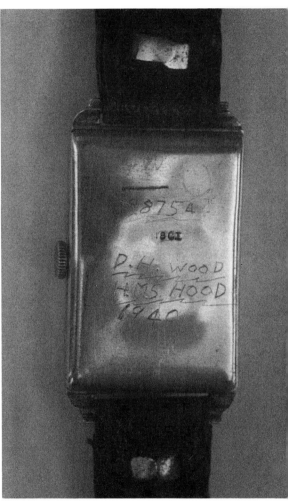

Prinz Eugen. During an engagement on 23 May a shell from *Bismark* penetrated *Hood's* aft magazine and she immediately blew up, sinking in three minutes with the loss of all but three of her complement of 1,419 men. At the time of writing it has not yet been established whether D.H.Wood was on board on 23 May 1941.
Value *£80-£100*

imor was a prolific supplier of the Army Time iece, circa 1939. They shared with all the other TPs produced by a variety of manufacturers the ame functional characteristics to meet the criteria f the military procurement programme. All had 15 ewel movements, luminous dials - mainly white, lthough some were available in black - waterproof ases, and fixed strap lugs for added security. This articular example of the Timor watch is still fitted vith its issue metal "Bonklip" bracelet.

waste, he was told that the Swiss watch companies contracted to supply the military sold their watches at reduced cost (achieved at times by the use of less expensive materials), on the condition that the Army contract watches were destroyed at the end of hostilities. This was in order to maintain the high reputation of their normal products and, more importantly, to avoid the flooding of the post-war commercial market with inexpensive Army surplus.

Inevitably, some watches did escape on to the

It seems almost incredible, but there is widespread evidence that of the many thousands of these watches which were produced, a high proportion were deliberately destroyed at the end of the war. One eyewitness in Italy watched in amazement as prisoners of war were given hammers and an anvil and set to methodically smashing watches one after another. When he questioned this astonishing

market, while others were put into storage - but these were to raise another difficulty. During the 1950s it was realised that large stocks of luminous timepieces were producing high levels of radiation; and once again the authorities set about destroying them, as radioactive waste.

Value £45-£50

In the 1940s Rotary advertised their watches with a
series of dramatic scenes from all branches of the
services and the claim that their timepieces were
good "For perfect split-second co-ordination".

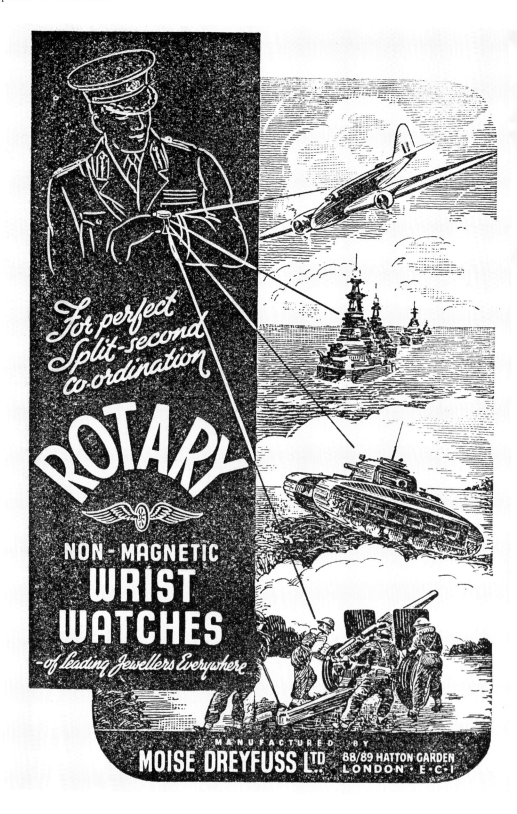

"Ordinary" wristwatches could not always be relied upon to withstand the opening shock and landing impact stresses imposed upon them during a Second World War military parachute descent; the strap might tear away from the lugs, or the watch might be rendered useless by a broken balance. By 1944 a watch specifically designed for the rigours of airborne work had been developed. Using existing stocks of Longines calibre 12.68N movements, which did not posses any shockproofing qualities, the research and development establishment of the War Department had constructed a special case to protect them. Made of brass nickel-plated with a satin finish, the waterproof case was made to a larger diameter than that of the movement; this allowed any violent shock to dissipate through the case rather than be transferred directly to the vulnerable movement. Other improvements included a rimmed glass which was inserted through the back of the watch and then secured by an "O" ring tightly screwed up behind it, eliminating any danger of the glass being knocked out of the case. Reinforced strap lugs were also provided. The screw back is engraved with the Company Ordnance Supply Depot (C.O.S.D.) abbreviation and the stores number "2131" (Paratrooper's Wristwatch); "2340" is the watch's serial number.

These watches were intended to be ready for issue by D-Day, 6 June 1944; however, even by the time of Operation Market Garden - the Arnhem drop - that September, many of these watches remained in various stages of incomplete assembly, and few were ever issued during the war. After the war most of the paratrooper's wristwatches were recalled to have new dials and hands fitted, which did away with the luminous paint used on the earlier issue model; in operational experience soldiers found that a severe impact could crack and powder the luminous paint, causing particles to accumulate beneath the glass, or to enter the movement and cause malfunctions.

Value £350-£450

During the period of the "phoney war" in the
West, 1939-40, which followed the invasion of
Poland, the Dutch military authorities began to pre-
pare themselves for all-out war. One of the minor
items of equipment procured in 1939 before the
German *blitzkrieg* broke over the Netherlands on 10
May 1940 were a number of Swiss-made wristwatches which were signed "Universal Geneve". These
black-dialled, luminous, 15 jewel timepieces were
marked on the dial with the Royal Crown over "W"
for the Dutch head of state Queen Wilhelmina.
Value *£80-£100*

Between 1933 and 1945 Kriegsmarine (German
Navy) issue timepieces were profusely marked with
the Nazi emblem; however, standard service wristwatches were only marked with the initials "KM".
Various Swiss and German manufacturers supplied
these wristwatches, which have several features in
common. Each has a white luminous dial with
Arabic numerals and subsidiary seconds. The
movements have 15 jewels and are housed in
waterproof, screw-back cases. This example is
signed Siegerin.
Value *£80-£100*

The number "592" which appears on the dial of this Kriegsmarine wristwatch has been used by the maker in place of their name. This number is in fact the calibre number of the movement, which attributes this piece to the Alpina watch company. This number is repeated on the 15 jewel movement.

Value *£80-£100*

German watchmakers produced only limited numbers of timepieces during the Second World War, the bulk of their efforts and capacity being devoted to the production of munitions fuses and timers. This economic utility wristwatch, issued to the Kriegsmarine circa 1943, is signed on the dial "Wagner". It is typical of the products produced for the home market. The movement, which is of baguette form, is made by the Urofa company and complies with the required 15 jewel standard. Although unorthodox for the watch's round case, the baguette shape does serve a purpose. Originally the case was designed for ease of manufacture and the back only has a snap fit. By distancing the movement from the side walls of the case the watch is still given some degree of waterproofing.

Value *£80-£100*

Prior to 1939 the German Wehrmacht demanded the best possible equipment for its troops, exploiting the latest technological advances. Even in the minor matter of timepieces, the armed forces were to have the most up-to-date products regardless of the extra costs. In 1933 various shock-resisting arrangements were being developed by the Swiss. Amongst these was the now universally famous "Incabloc" system. All the various methods worked by having the balance cock jewel sprung. This allowed a degree of axial movement to the balance, minimising the risk of damage to the pivots from shock. By 1938 a variety of these systems had been improved to the extent that they could be offered in all watch calibres. Realising the benefits, the Wehrmacht procurement authorities stipulated that all subsequent contracts with the Swiss should specify shockproof wristwatches. This example, signed "Glycine", is typical of the type of standard wristwatch supplied to the German Army circa 1940. The watch uses a movement supplied by the Swiss ebauche maker A.Schild, identifiable by the calibre number A.S.1130.

Value *£60-£80*

Not all German Army suppliers used the A.S.1130 movement. As long as the wristwatch offered the desired features - a shock-resistant movement with a minimum of 15 jewels; faced strap lugs, to prevent the wristwatch from being wrenched off the arm; a waterproof case, and a luminous dial - it was acceptable as a service timepiece. This is one such example made by Revue, retailed as their "Sport" model, which was accepted by the Wehrmacht circa 1940. Here Revue have used their own calibre 59 movement which employs the "Incabloc" shock protecting system. Other suppliers who used alternative movements include, amongst others, Longines, Titus and Zenith.
Value *£60-£80 (Revue),*
£150 -£180 (Longines),
£70-£80 (Titus),
£120-£150 (Zenith)

Among the numerous manufacturers who supplied the German Army with their standard issue wrist-watches were Cronos, this example dating from circa 1940. Notwithstanding the name on the dial, so many of these companies assembled watches using calibre A.S.1130 movements that this was frequently referred to simply as the "Wehrmacht" movement.

Value *£60-£80*

Despite the fact that these three German Army wristwatches of Second World War date are all made by different Swiss companies, they exhibit certain common characteristics. Firstly, all are sealed in waterproof cases; secondly, all these cases take a single pattern of six-pronged spanner to remove the screw back; and thirdly, each is fitted with fixed strap lugs.

Because the Swiss companies did not supply their watches to the Wehrmacht exclusively - indeed, the majority of similar wristwatches were retailed worldwide on a commercial basis - the need arose to identify the Swiss-made Wehrmacht issue pieces. A "DH" for Deutsches Heer (German Army) property mark was stamped onto the screw back with a variety of different die stamps; numerous typefaces are encountered, varying both in style and size. The serial number was typically marked between the "D" and the "H", as on these examples.

The wartime German watch companies had no need to mark the watches which they supplied with the "DH" stamp. The industry was under government control, and any wristwatches that were produced were solely for the use of the Wehrmacht. Since there could never be any dispute as to their ownership the need to mark them never arose.

In times of shortage, the German watchmaking industry supplied the Army with an economic "utility" wristwatch. These watches, such as this example by Wagner circa 1942, used a 15 jewel Urofa movement of baguette form. This movement offered none of the shockproofing that the Swiss timepieces provided, and was housed in a snap-back case (see the KM issue Wagner watch, page 70). There are no property markings on these watches.
Value £40 -£50

RA PD 78880

Figure 112 — Hamilton Wrist Watch, 17-jewel, 6/0 Size — Front and Back

Figure 112 in TM 9-1575 depicts Hamilton's 17 jewel Model 987A wristwatch. Originally produced in 1937, with its white dial and subsidiary seconds hand, this watch was issued to both the US Army and Navy, in a snap-back case marked either "ORD. DEPT. U.S.A." or "U.S.N. Bu of Ships". By 1940 the design was changed to a screw-back waterproof case. Hamilton also supplied 3,000 units of the Model 987A to the Russian military authorities between 1942 and 1945. Production of this watch carried on throughout the Korean War period. The post-1945 model has a case made of either stainless steel or with a protective parkerized finish. The case design also appears to be of a more angular form, particularly in the areas of the strap lugs.
Value *£90-£100*

Hamilton upgraded the specification of their 987A movement, circa 1939, by adding a centre seconds hand and a hacking device. This latest movement was known as the 987S and had either 17 or 18 jewels. As with all Hamilton products, these watches were manufactured to a meticulous standard of quality, and consequently production figures were low when compared with the volume produced by other companies. Hamilton's records show that the total of 987S watches produced over the years 1940-1945 came to only 38,298; these were issued to the US Navy and US Marine Corps. However, a further 2,000 were made under contract for the Royal Canadian Air Force.

Figure 126 in the TM shows the 7 jewel Grade 580 and 15 jewel Grade 554 Elgin wristwatches. These are shown in their original form, with snapback cases, as issued to the US Navy; a smaller number were also procured for the US Army. By 1940 a waterproof case had been added to the specification. Originally a two-piece leather strap was fitted to these watches; however, in practice it was found that during sea duty the leather rapidly perished. On occasion a green canvas strap was provided, but this too proved to be unsuitable for the extreme climatic conditions of the Pacific. To combat the problem a one-piece safety strap was developed especially for the US Marine Corps, made of rot-proof moulded nylon.

Value *£50-£60 (Grade 580), £65-£75 (Grade 554)*

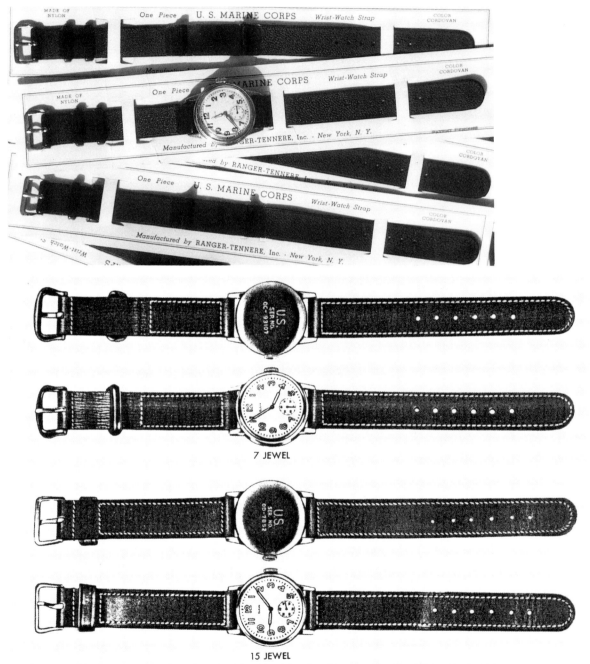

7 JEWEL

15 JEWEL

RA PD

Figure 126 — Elgin Wrist Watches — 7- and 15-jewel, 8/0 Size — Front and Back

gure 144 clearly illustrates the manner of attach-
g the Elgin Grade 539 wristwatch to the safety
rap. Note the ordnance marking "OFA" on the
ack of the decagonal waterproof case, suggesting
e by US Army ground troops.

Figure 150 shows the 9 jewel Model 10609 Waltham
wristwatch, which was available from 1942. The
wristwatch is shown with a three-piece dustproof case.
No tools are required for opening the back; there is a
reeded edge to ease turning of the bezel and case back
by hand. When the waterproof case was introduced a
special decagonal spanner was required to remove the
gasket-sealed back. **Value** *£70-£80*

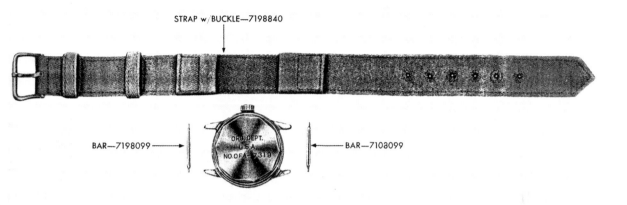

STRAP w/BUCKLE—7198840

BAR—7198099   BAR—7108099

RA PD 78984

Figure 144 — Elgin Wrist Watch — Wrist Band Removed

BACK

FRONT

RA PD 78961

Figure 150 — Waltham Wrist Watch, 9-jewel, 6/0 Size — Front and Back

Figure 165 illustrates the waterproof 15 jewel
Model 10AK US Army issue Bulova wristwatch.
These watches were built in the USA, circa 1940,
although the original designs were Swiss. The screw
back is marked "ORD DEPT USA" above a serial
and "BULOVA WATCH CO."
Vague *£70-£80*

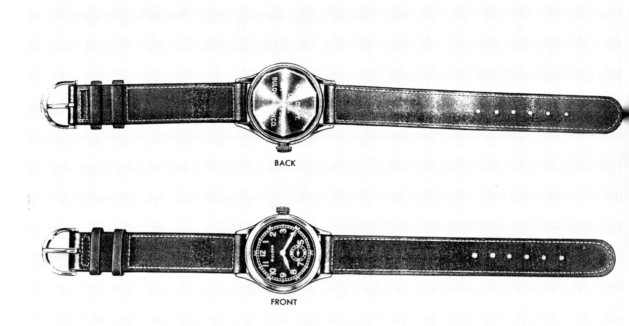

BACK

FRONT

RA PD 78979

Figure 165 — Bulova Wrist Watch — 15-jewel, 10½ Ligne Size — Front and Back

oduction of the 15 jewel Bulova Model 10AK
rried on into the 1950s. This example from circa
953 is marked to the rear of the waterproof case
DRD CORPS USA", while the serial number is
refixed with the "OF" code. The post-war case is
ade from steel treated with the chemical process
nown as "parkerizing"; this gives the case anti-cor-
sive properties and is characterised by a dark grey
pearance to the metal. The case design also dif-
rs, most noticeably around the strap lugs, which
ave been machined to form a more angular
pearance than found on the earlier pattern.
alue *£70-£80*

Towards the end of the Second World War the War Department procured the first serious military wristwatches destined for the British armed forces. The designers of this new breed of timepiece, known as the "Wristwatch, Waterproof" i military terminology (and marked "W.W.W."), had taken into account many of the most desirable features for a service watch and combined them into one product. A variety of makers were then responsible for assembling these watches, which had few external differences. The chief specifications were that they should have clear, black, luminous dials; proven 15 jewel movements capable of delivering an excellent level of accuracy, over a wide variety of conditions; subsidiary seconds dials; tough shatterproof perspex glass; rugged case design capable of diminishing the results of shock to the movement (oddly, the movements themselves still had no shock-resisting device fitted); a higher than normal level of waterproofing, and a water-resistant winding crown of good size. Among the first of these wristwatches to be made available were those supplied by Timor and Omega, circa 1944. Other brands followed, including Buren, Cyma, Eterna International Watch Company, Jaeger Le Coultre, Lemania, Record and Vertex. A number of these companies carried on delivering watches well into the 1950s.

Value *£50-£60 (Timor), £60 -£70 (Buren), £80 -£100 (Cyma), £70-£80 (Eterna), £450-£500 (International), £200-£250 (Jaeger Le Coultre), £60-£70 (Lemania), £100-£120 (Omega), £50-£60 (Record), £60-£70 (Vertex).*

Advertisement from the 1950s, when Vertex
launched their latest waterproof wristwatch on the
commercial market.

Longines are no strangers to the challenge of developing watches especially suited to the polar environment; as early as 1899 the firm had supplied Luigi Amadeo, Duke of Abruzzi, with a series of chronometer watches for his expedition to the North Pole. Following this success Longines were approached on several other occasions to supply watches for such expeditions (e.g. Captain Bernier's voyage to the Arctic in 1905, and Admiral Byrd's three expeditions to the Antarctic in the 1930s.)

It is not surprising that in 1953 Longines should have developed this wristwatch for a series of British military scientific expeditions to the Arctic regions. The 15 jewel movement was a refined Longines calibre 12.68Z, which had a "shock-resist" system fitted. The rugged stainless steel case is marked with the Waterproof Wristwatch abbreviation.
Value *£350-£400*

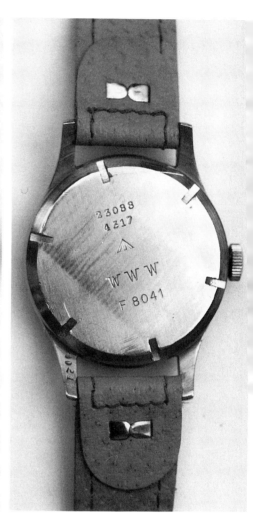

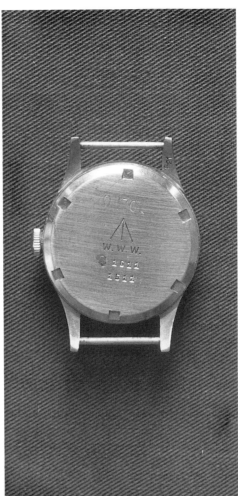

The British Army issue Invicta waterproof wristwatch appeared circa 1960. Unusually for this pattern of watch a white dial has been used, with each
numeral picked out in tritium paint, as opposed to
the simple luminous marks found on the more
usual black dial. The subsidiary seconds dial has
been omitted. The movement itself has 17 jewels
and an Incabloc device. The screw back bears the
"WWW" and broad arrow mark.
Value *£50-£60*

In the 1970s the CWC company produced a
tonneau-shaped wristwatch in a monobloc case.
This is reminiscent of the original concept devised
by Borgel and used in many of the First World
War military pattern early waterproof wristwatches;
access to the movement is gained from the front
after removing the armoured perspex glass. Most of
these CWC models, like this example, bear the
British Army issue "W10" prefix to the rear of the
case. A special feature of this watch is the hacking
device which has been fitted, to stop the centre
seconds hand during time setting. An identical
wristwatch was also produced by Hamilton of
Geneva, which used the same ebauche as in the
CWC model. Most of the Hamilton wristwatches
were used by the Royal Air Force and are engraved
on the back with the "6bb" prefix.

Production of the CWC wristwatch continued
for several years until a quartz model, again
supplied by CWC, superseded the mechanical
watch. However, a mechanical watch identical to
the CWC in appearance only became available to
armed forces stationed in Germany circa 1989.
This latest model, supplied by MWC, was basically
a "throw-away" watch, with a 1 jewel pin pallet
movement. All these modern standard wristwatches
are frequently referred to by military personnel as
"G-Ten Ninety-Eights", from the Form G-10/98
which accompanies the requisition request for the
issue of service equipment.
Value *£45-£50 (CWC),*
£70-£80 (Hamilton),
£30-£40 (MWC),
£40-£50 (CWC Quartz)

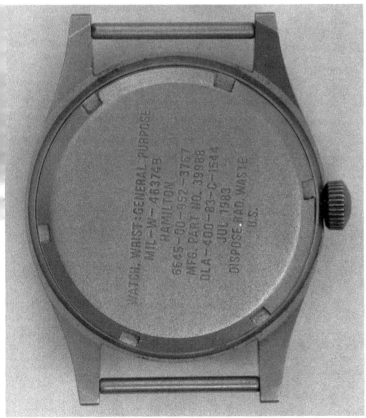

Hamilton produced this "WATCH, WRIST: GENERAL PURPOSE" for the US Army circa 1983; this example is dated on the six-notch screw back "JUL.1983". It conforms to military requirements as laid down under specification number "MIL-W-463748", which also appears on the back. Note also, on the face, the small radioactive symbol together with "H3", denoting the properties of the luminous material used in the manufacture of the dial. While one wristwatch does not pose a health threat, large stockpiles of these timepieces would be hazardous. To alert personnel to this potential danger the back of this watch is further marked "DISPOSE RAD. WASTE".

Value *£50-£60*

Originally these Russian "Kommanderski" wristwatches were produced by Wostock in the early
1980s for military personnel to purchase from military outfitters. Since then numerous wristwatches
have been produced with a variety of different dial
designs depicting various military emblems or
insignia. Both the illustrated examples - with a
green and a black face respectively, and with red
and black infilled engraving on the rotating bezels -
bear the Airborne Forces insignia surmounted by
the Communist red star. In today's youth culture
such watches have become popular as ironic fash-
ion accessories and, due to the lifting of the Iron
Curtain, they are readily available on the commercial market in vast quantities.

Value *£15-£20*

This Wostock Kommanderski wristwatch features on its attractive royal blue luminous dial a fouled anchor motif together with the image of a submarine; naturally, the red star is also present at the 12 o'clock location. Other features found in these watches include a rotating bezel, a calendar facility and a waterproof screw-down winding crown, which is protected from knocks by high shoulders on the side of the case.
Value *£15-£20*

All the Kommanderski wristwatches made by Wostock have employed their 17 jewel movement, fitted into a waterproof case made of either chromed or gilt brass. Predominantly it is only the emblems applied to the faces that differ from model to model; this example features a tank.
Value *£15-£20*

OBSERVATION & AVIATOR'S WRISTWATCHES

While Lieutenant-Commander Philip Van Horn Weems, US Navy, was an instructor in aerial navigation at Annapolis in 1927, he realised that aviators faced serious problems under the conditions met in fast aircraft. At speeds of 200mph an aeroplane would cover one mile every 18 seconds; and any delay in navigational calculations, coupled with unavoidable chronometer error, might well be compounded to a hazardous degree. To counter this Weems offered a simple solution to the problem of chronometer error. He designed a wristwatch with a rotatable subsidiary dial in the centre of the face, which could be synchronised to the sweeping seconds hand against a time signal. This method was preferred to employing a hacking device, as watchmakers were of the opinion that continual interference with the balance adversely effected its timekeeping qualities. In use, the navigator could adjust the dial on the Weems watch to counter any known error over the duration of the flight; for example, for a known chronometer error rate of 12 seconds per day the navigator would make an adjustment of plus/minus four seconds during an eight-hour flight.

This large wristwatch was produced in America by the Longines-Wittnauer company using the 15 jewel calibre 37.9 movement, at a cost of $80 each. It then went into service under the designation Type A-3 pilot's watch in 1932, remaining on issue until 1943. The Japanese Navy obtained a quantity of these watches for their airmen; and paradoxically, on 7 December 1941 some might well have been worn by Mitsuo Fuchida's crews in the skies over Pearl Harbor. (Courtesy Sotheby's)
Value *£2,800-£3,000*

zechoslovak Air Force pilots, circa 1938, were
sued with oversized Longines wristwatches
hich were worn on a leather band around the
uff of the uniform tunic. The earliest examples
these unusually styled wristwatches employed
ue 15 jewel Longines calibre 15.94 movement,
hich had its origins in 1904. Later this was
anged to calibre 15.26, but by 1939 Longines
ere supplying these watches with their most
odern calibre 15.68Z movements, which were

ewelled to the centre. Importantly, the last two
movements were designed to have anti-magnetic
properties - a valuable attribute in the cockpit of
an aeroplane, surrounded by equipment of an
electromagnetic nature. A painted dial had by
now also replaced the older enamel face, which
had an unfortunate tendency to shatter under a
sharp blow. A rotating marker bezel was also common to all models.

To fulfil the urgent need for these timepieces
the Czechoslovak authorities issued the first
batches of Longines wristwatches without waiting
to apply property marks. Then, as supply caught
up with demand, remaining stores of these watches were serially numbered with the running total
and engraved with the military inscription
"MAJETEK VOJENSKE SPRAVY". It is believed
that only about 3,000 Longines wristwatches were
supplied to the Czechoslovak Air Force.
Value *£500-£600*

This example of the Czechoslovak Air Force
Longines wristwatch, circa 1939, has been
engraved by hand with initials and "za letecke [for
air force use] Longines". The movement in this
instance is the 17 jewel calibre 15.68Z.
(Courtesy J.Dowling)
Value *£500-£600*

The Lemania Watch Company, circa 1939, provided the Czechoslovak Air Force with a wristwatch not unlike the Longines model in style. After the outbreak of war many of these watches were re-routed and made their way to England, to serve with the various Czech squadrons throughout the Royal Air Force, such as No.311 (Bomber) Squadron. These watches feature a waterproof screw-back case containing the 17 jewel movement fitted with Incabloc shock protection, and a central sweeping seconds hand which made the watch more suitable for navigational or observation purposes. Eterna also supplied an identical wristwatch. **Value** *£300-£350 (Lemania), £300-£350 (Eterna)*

In the early Nazi years, during the mid-1930s, this pattern of aviator's wristwatch was being retailed in Germany. Signed on the dial "NATALIS", this oversized wristwatch is unusual in that it still uses a 15 jewel cylinder movement; cylinder escapements were not known for their accuracy, and had all but been superceded by the vastly superior lever escapements by 1920. Perhaps the watchmaker was making economical use of old stock movements? Nevertheless, the watch does have some excellent characteristics. It has a black 24-hour luminous dial protected beneath a 3mm thick crystal glass, and a rotatable marker bezel which can be used to note starting times, etc., plus a large winding crown which is effective when used with gloved hands.
Value *£100 -£150*

Helvetia, amongst other companies, produced avia-
ors' wristwatches circa 1938. Retailed in Germany,
hese had 15 jewel shock-protected movements.
Note also the propeller motif below the company
ame on the dial. They were designed to be worn
round the sleeve of a flying suit and had broad lugs
which allowed the fitting of a strong leather strap.
An example of this type of wristwatch was reputedly
ound to have been worn by a crewman of a Heinkel
He111 bomber during the Battle of Britain.
Value *£150-£200*

Observation watches were a speciality of Lange & Sohne, who produced these large, quality wristwatches for the Luftwaffe circa 1939, using a pocket watch movement with centre seconds. These watches were worn around the arm of the flying clothing on long leather straps (and not around the leg, as has been suggested). The fully luminous dial has an inner 12-hour ring read by reference to the short stubby hour hand, while the circumference is graduated for the seconds and numbered at every five-minute point. It is apparent that the dial layout was designed to giv aircrew greater access to the elapsing minutes an seconds. Prior to a flight the navigator would set his watch to the second, by means of the balance stopping device operated when the winder is pulled out during hand setting. Other manufacturers of this watch included Internatior Watch Company (who only produced 1,200), Laco, Stowa and Wempe.

ter the war these watches were produced in East
ermany by the newly established GUB works.
Courtesy Sotheby's)
alue *£700-£800 (Lange & Sohne),
,800-£2,000 (International), £500-£600 (Laco,
owa), £450-£500 (Wempe), £400-£450 (GUB)*

The standard wristwatches issued to the German
Army were also available to the Luftwaffe.
However, it was believed that their general issue
was inappropriate; the Luftwaffe had special
purpose watches to fulfill all their requirements,
and anything else would be superfluous. Any
aircrew who desired wristwatches of their own
could purchase them direct from the stores. These
wristwatches are distinguished by a "D" for Dienst
serial number prefix on the back of the case,
identifying them as being of "service" grade, a
guarantee of excellence.

Value *(Same as for Army issue watches, pages 71-74)*

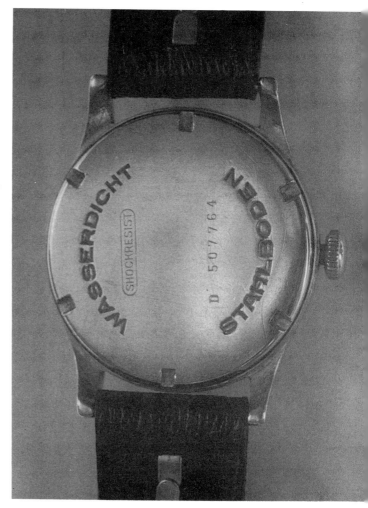

LONGINES WATCHES
(from all leading Jewellers)

THE WATCH
FOR THE
NAVY, ARMY & AIR FORCE

10 GRANDS PRIX

LONGINES supremacy, due to superior workmanship, asserts itself wherever watches are put to the most exacting tests, as shown by the number of Highest Awards won at all important exhibitions held since 1867.

SEE THAT THE NAME IS ON THE MOVEMENT

LONGINES WATCHES were used exclusively or were selected after tests as the Official Timepieces for over 28 important flights from 1926 up to date

such as

ROUND THE WORLD	- -	Post and Gatty, Graf Zeppelin
ACROSS THE ATLANTIC	Lindbergh, Kingsford-Smith, Miss Earhart	
ACROSS THE PACIFIC	- - -	Herndorn and Pangborn
POLAR EXPEDITIONS	- - -	Nobile, Byrd, Williams

In 1923 Longines had been adopted as the official timer for the world's aviation record attempts. Their enviable reputation as an innovative watch-making company was further enhanced through their association with famous pioneering aviation figures. At the time when Longines produced this advertisement in the 1933 edition of the Royal Air Force "Manual of Air Force Law" they were still in their heyday, garlanded by association with numerous recent aviation achievements.

In 1939 a small number of commercial grade Rolex wristwatches were procured for the Fleet Air Arm, so identified by the "HS-8" marking on the back of the cushion-form snap-back case. Ordinarily, despite the pedigree, this watch would not have met the specification requirements for a pilot's issue wristwatch. In this instance the fact that the watch only has a small subsidiary seconds dial has been overlooked. Perhaps an attitude of wartime "making do", and the fact that the watch was not going to be used for any navigational purpose, may have swayed the FAA into accepting this watch. In all other respects this Rolex, with its 15 jewel movement, is an admirable military timepiece.
Value *£500-£600*

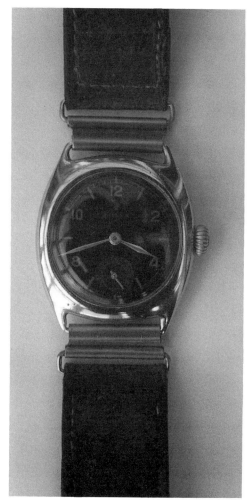

While this Fleet Air Arm issue Omega wristwatch may appear identical to its Royal Air Force counterpart, it does have certain minor but relevant differences. This watch, which bears the Hydrographic Service mark, has a nickel-plated brass case, which replaced the solid nickel case as an economy measure circa 1940. As a compromise, the FAA found that the brass cases still offered some protection against sea corrosion. Removable sprung strap bars were also permitted on the FAA wristwatches. By 1942, due to shortages, the FAA were forced into using the same cheap alloy-cased watches as the RAF, although these were not resistant to long term corrosion on sea duty.
Value £100-£120

Whenever any military equipment is issued an
entry is made in the recipient's personal papers.
This "Flying Clothing Card" was given to
Lieutenant L.W.A.Lee, Royal Naval Reserve. Lee
was a naval airman, and on 25 June 1945 he was
issued with his HS8 wristwatch, serial number
10400, details of which have been recorded on
page 6 of the document.

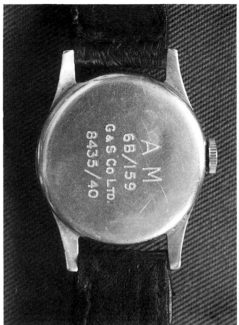

In 1939 the Goldsmith's & Silversmith's Company Limited approached Longines to supply them with a quantity of airmen's watches. These used a 16 jewel calibre 10.68N movement, which made the overall size of this wristwatch smaller than the normal Royal Air Force issue timepiece (cf. the Omega, below). However, in this time of crisis and in order to meet the high demand for wristwatches, the Air Ministry were only too delighted to accept these into service. Prior to issue the back of the watch was engraved with the usual AM property marks, codes and 1940 date, together with the details of the supplier.

Value *£120-£150*

The Weems system of setting the seconds hand to
the exact time has been simplified in this smaller
wristwatch produced in 1940. A rotatable bezel is
turned by hand until synchronised against a time
signal; the bezel is then locked in place by the
screw button in the 4 o'clock position. This
example, beautifully marked and in excellent
condition, was made by Omega and supplied to
the RAF by the Goldsmith's & Silversmith's
Company Ltd. It was designated by the Air
Ministry as a Mk VIIA and coded 6B 159,
identifying it as having been issued to pilots and
navigators. The back of this watch has also been
personalised at some stage by its user, F.A.Wuras,
who engraved his details including his date of birth
as 01.11.1917. Other manufacturers of the Weems
patent watch included Jaeger Le Coultre, Longines,
Movado and Zenith.
Value *£400-£500 (Omega, Longines),*
£450-£550 (Jaeger Le Coultre, Movado, Zenith)

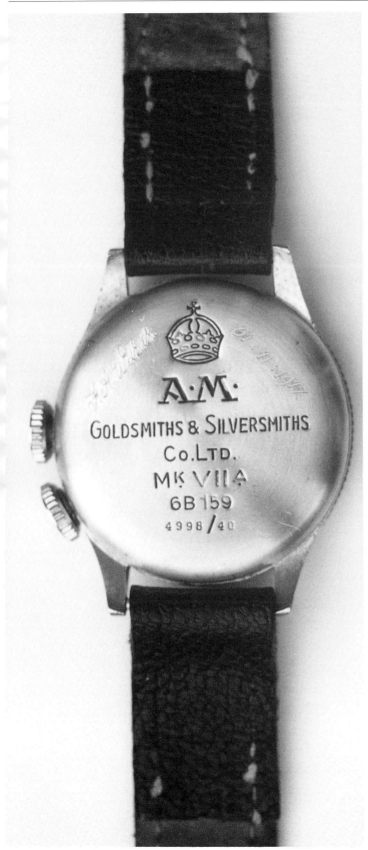

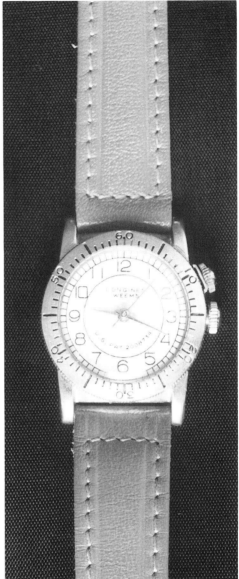

Above An even smaller Weems wristwatch was produced in 1940 by Longines; although it was primarily intended for civilian use, a small number were acquired by the Royal Air Force. (It is known that at least one such watch was issued to the navigator of a Lancaster bomber in 1942.) The back of this nickel-cased watch bears no issue marks, but the dial is signed both LONGINES and WEEMS. It bears the US patent number 2008734, which was granted to P.V.H.Weems for his original design on 31 July 1935. A gold-filled version was also retailed on the commercial market. The back of these watches is dedicated "Lt.Com.P.V.H.Weems U.S.N. Longines Weems Seconds Setting Watch". **Value** *£250-£300, £300-£350 (gold-filled)*

This early nickel-cased Omega wristwatch, circa 1940, bears Royal Air Force flying equipment code numbers. Interestingly, it is also engraved with the initials "P.A.F.", indicating issue to the Polish Air Force serving under the auspices of the Royal Air Force. This wristwatch employs Omega's 16 jewel calibre 30 T2 SC movement. After 1940 these watches no longer used the nickel case, being fitted into soft alloy "economy" cases. The author obtained this watch from an antique dealer near Northolt, the wartime base of the Polish Nos.302 and 303 (Fighter) Squadrons, RAF.
Value *£200-£250*

A number of Cyma timepieces were used by the
British Army both as pocket and wristwatches. This
example, however, is a private purchase wristwatch
which differs from the Army Timepiece only in
lacking a luminous dial, and in having removable
spring lug bars which permit the use of the full
range of commercial straps and bracelets. In all other

respects, including the 15 jewel movement, it is the same as those issued for ATP use. Interestingly, the screw back on this Cyma bears a presentation inscription to Sergeant Selfe, who served on a Royal Air Force Officer Cadet Training Unit. It reads, "SGT. SELFE FROM M.G. WING 162ND O.C.T.U. (H.A.C.) 13.1.40". *Value £80-£100*

In 1940 the Air Ministry began the issue of "economy" wristwatches. These were meant for use under circumstances where the expense of the high quality "known brand" watches could not be justified; the latter remained primarily for issue to the navigators. Although the unsigned economy watches performed their function adequately, they lacked the prestige that the pilots looked for, despite having the same features as their more desirable counterparts: 15 jewel Swiss movements, and white dials

with blued steel hands including central sweeping seconds. The back of this nickel-cased watch is marked with the Air Ministry code "14.A/1102", identifying it as having been used for reconnaissance duties. Others of this type are to be found with "6B" issue codes. Use of these watches was short-lived after supplies of the brand name watches resumed in the new economy alloy cases.
Value *£60-£70*

his peculiar-looking timepiece, which is designat-
 on the case "14A/82", is part of an RAF air-
aft's photographic reconnaissance equipment.
efore take-off the photo-recce camera would be
aded with a new roll of film, and this timepiece
ould be set to the correct time before being
ounted into the camera. As the pilot flew over his
rget location he would operate the camera, and
hile the lens shutter operated a photo record was
ade of the actual time on the negative. This

assisted the Air Intelligence Branch interpreters
during their scrutiny of the developed photographs. The watch itself contains an unsigned 15
jewel movement of the type that was used in the
economy wristwatch, circa 1941.
Value *£45-£50*

Longines was the second most prolific maker of wristwatches to the Royal Air Force. Their offering employed the 16 jewel calibre 12.68N movement, which was made available from 1939. Note also the dial on this example, which uses classic italic numerals rather than the more usual printed standard block numerals. The use of the economy alloy case and the civilian pattern dial suggest that the watch dates from 1941. Unusually, this watch appears to be unissued, as it has retained its original unlined pigskin strap sewn on to the strap lugs and shows no sign of wear. (Courtesy D.Penny) **Value** *£200-£250 (unissued)*

The Air Ministry considered the issue of waterproof wristwatches for use in the confines of an aircraft cockpit of no value and unnecessarily expensive. However, circa 1941-43 Jaeger Le Coultre were producing one of the war's finest wristwatches for issue to the Royal Air Force. Construction of these watches, together with the materials used, was of such quality that while the case only had a snap-on back its fit was so good that it provided for a high degree of water-resistance. Jaeger Le Coultre refused to have their watches compromised in any way and, while others supplied economy alloy cases, these watches were only available with a plated brass case. Even in small details Jaeger Le Coultre looked to stand above all other companies' products, e.g. by supplying their watches with their unique style of blue steel hands.

Value *£180-£200*

In 1940 this large wristwatch was issued to Red
Army officers and pilots. The watch is of Russian
manufacture and, in keeping with other Russian
military timepieces, the date "3-40" has been
stamped above the serial number on the movement. With the subsidiary seconds dial being in
the 9 o'clock position, it is apparent that a 15 jewel
pocket watch movement has been utilised in the
production of these pieces. In appearance these
wristwatches differ very little from the ones issued
to the Czar's Imperial Air Force pre-1918. Those
early examples are of superior quality and have
dials signed by the Swiss maker "Moser & Cie".
Both types have pressed sheet steel cases, which
were chromed and fitted with articulated strap
lugs. Early timepieces have no property marks,
while those in service after the 1918 Bolshevik
Revolution were engraved with the "CCCP"
mark when time allowed.
Value *£140-£160*

In 1942 Movado supplied a small quantity of
wristwatches to the Air Ministry; featuring their 15
jewel calibre 75 movement, these are among the
rarest of the RAF issue watches produced during
the war. Unlike the other RAF wristwatches of this
period, the white dial has its chapter ring marked
from 5 to 60 at five-second intervals, while each
seconds graduation is divided into fifths. Another
scarce version of the RAF wristwatch was manufactured by Ebel. **Value** *£180-£200*

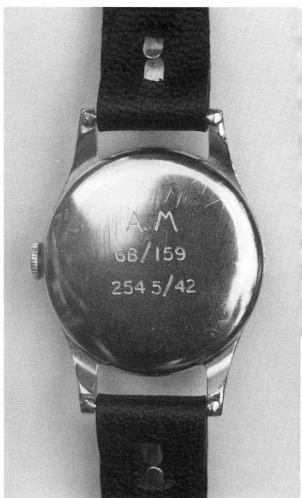

The Seikosha watch company supplied a large wristwatch for pilots of the Imperial Japanese Navy, circa 1941. Worn around the sleeve of the flying suit, these featured a black luminous dial. The outer chapter ring was graduated in seconds and numbered up to 60 at five-second intervals. This chapter ring could be rotated by means of the outer bezel, which had a heavily reeded edge for ease of use even with gloved hands. By using this bezel the pilot could synchronise the seconds hand to the exact time. Setting the watch hands was made easier by the enlarged winding crown. The back of this watch is marked with Japanese characters amongst which is the symbol of an anchor. (Courtesy Sotheby's)

Value *£900-£1,000*

The 17 jewel Waltham Model 10617 wristwatch was first made available in 1942. It differed from the 9 jewel Model 10609 in having a black dial, centre seconds hand, and a hacking device. As with this example, the first timepieces off the production line were fitted into dustproof cases, but this was later changed to the waterproof type of case. They were variously engraved, either with "TYPE A11" specification details or "USN BUSHIPS".

Unlike the Army models which had hands of a skeletal form, which relied upon surface tension to keep the luminous paint in place, the flyer's wristwatches used a solid hand with a thin adhesive luminous coating, of a pale cream colour, applied over their surface. Although the luminous properties were impaired by this process, it reduced the danger of the luminous material crumbling and particles falling into the movement. Naturally, the Army relied on timepieces being highly visible at night and in consequence they were unable to accept watches with their hands luminised in this alternative manner.

Value *£80-£100*

igure 142 in the technical manual illustrates the
6 jewel Grade 539 Elgin wristwatch; this features
central sweeping seconds hand, a waterproof case
nd a hacking device. It was primarily intended for
sue to US Army Air Corps/Air Forces and US
lavy pilots, but large numbers found their way
nto the hands of ground troops. These can be dif-
rentiated by the inscription "ORD. DEPT.
I.S.A.". Elgin, ever mindful of the problems
ncountered by pilots at high altitude, developed a
ynthetic watch oil with very low solidification
roperties which allowed the watch to function
ven in temperatures as low as -50 degrees F. The
atch is shown attached to one of the green canvas
afety straps. In the 1950s Elgin improved the
ilot's wristwatch by creating an 18 jewel Grade
85 movement, which became the Type A-17A
sued to the US Air Force.

alue *£80 -£100 (Grade 539), £80-£90-(Grade 685)*

BACK

FRONT

RA PD 78945

Figure 142 — Elgin Wrist Watch — 16-jewel, 8/0 Size — Front and Back

In 1942 Waltham were contracted to supply the
Royal Canadian Air Force with their new 16 jewel
Model 10616-C-S-12 wristwatches. Apart from
some cosmetic changes to the dial and hands this
rare RCAF version was the same as the US Army
Air Forces' Type A-11 wristwatch. A waterproof
case was used, which was engraved with Air
Ministry flying equipment codes. Each wristwatch
cost a total of $13.64 and came with a two-piece
olive green canvas strap.
Value *£180-£200*

The wristwatch which evolved from the Model 10AK was an improved Model 10AKCSH. Basically this latest Bulova wristwatch had a 16 jewel movement and a central sweeping seconds hand, plus a hacking device. It became designated as the Type A-11, as can be seen on the profusely engraved back, which also bears details of specification and part numbers. From the first two digits of the Air Forces' "AF"-prefixed serial number the date of the watch can be identified - in this case 1943 from "AF43 70456". Many more of these watches were also issued to pilots serving under the US Navy Bureau of Aeronautics. During 1942 many of these wristwatches were also issued to the Royal Air Force.

Value *£80-£100*

In 1953 the RAF took delivery of the latest offering from Omega, whose 17 jewel calibre 283 movement proved to be a great success. It was robust, shockproof (with Incabloc), accurate and aesthetically pleasing. The waterproof screw-back case, of large proportions, is deeply stamped with NATO stores numbers coupled with RAF "6B" flying equipment codes and a broad arrow, which also appears on the dial. Behind the screw back a separate dust cover gives added protection to the movement. These watches were not issued in any other year.
Value *£180–£200*

Following Bulova's successful Type A-11 the company refined their wristwatch still further. In the 1950s they upgraded the movement to 17 jewels and added an Incabloc shockproof system. Now known as the Model 10BNCH, this latest wristwatch was accepted for issue to the US Air Force as the Type A-17A. An inner chapter ring numbered from 13 to 24 was marked at each hourly interval, to aid use with the military timekeeping system. This particular example has retained its original green nylon webbing strap.
Value *£80–£90*

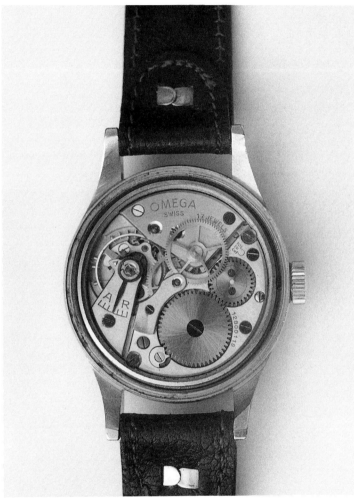

CHRONOGRAPHS, INTERVAL TIMERS & STOP WATCHES

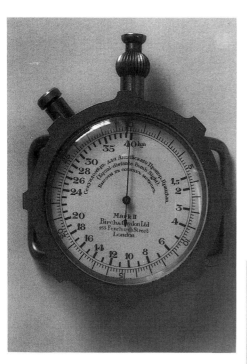

In 1917 the American Expeditionary Forces purchased 3,000 Vacheron & Constantin chronograph pocket watches for issue to the Corps of Engineers. The sterling silver case houses a fine quality 20 jewel movement that will run for 36 hours on one winding. To guarantee accuracy it was adjusted for isochronism, temperature and three positions. Other refinements include a swan neck micrometer regulator and Breguet hair spring. The centre second chronograph was activated by pressing the button in the winding crown. Subsequent pressing would stop and reset the interval timer. The outer seconds chapter ring is graduated in fifths of a second for precise measurement. Other examples may be found with red 24-hour markings on the dial. **Value** *£800-£1,000*

During the First World War, squadrons from the Royal Naval Air Service went to Russia to assist the Czar's air force; and among the equipment they took with them was this fascinating Mark II timer. Supplied by Birch & Gaydon of London, circa 1914, this watch was specially commissioned for the Russian expeditionary force, as is evident from the bilingual Russian Cyrillic and English script on the dial, which reads "Equal-distance Bomb Sight". This timer was worn around the sleeve of the flying suit (note the large, robust lugs) and used in conjunction with the aforementioned bomb sight. The timer had a complicated movement which permitted the centre hand to run forwards (clockwise) until, with a further depression of the plunger extending from the winding crown, the mechanism could be halted, and the button to the left pressed to engage the mechanism to run backwards (anticlockwise), when commencing a bombing run.
Value *£300-£400*

During the period of political, social and economic
chaos which plagued Germany in the aftermath of
the First World War the weak Weimar Republic -
whose authority was threatened by armed extremist
groups - was obliged to maintain defensive forces.
Ever wary of criticism, the government began slow-
ly to re-equip their Navy (Reichsmarine), considering this to be the "safe" political option. Money
was in very short supply, and consequently so was
the new equipment. This timepiece is a rare
Reichsmarine issue chronograph pocket watch dating from circa 1929. To reduce the cost only the
fine quality 17 jewel movement was imported,
from the Swiss company Minerva; the silver double
snap-back watch case was manufactured and hall-
marked in Germany. The chronograph mechanism
was started, stopped and reset by subsequent
depressions of the button in the top winder. The
white enamel dial had a 30-minute register; and to
make the watch compatible with the military 24-
hour time system (which was in widespread use
throughout Europe), an inner chapter ring, marking the hours 13-24 in red, was added. The eagle
over "M" was the Reichsmarine property mark
until 1933, when the style of the eagle changed
and the swastika was adopted.

Value *£450-£500*

Lemania has a long association with the military, and the various chronograph watches which they supplied circa 1914-1960 are highly regarded. This early example of a pocket chronograph, circa 1938, bears the Royal Navy pattern of broad arrow on the rear of the nickel snap-back case housing the 17 jewel movement. The chronograph is operated by depressing the winder and is capable of measuring time intervals of up to 30 minutes on the separate register dial, while the chapter ring is calibrated in fifths of a second for precise time calculations.

Value *£100-£120*

The Kriegsmarine Artillerietrager were allocated three pocket chronograph watches per unit, of which this is one example. Made by Leonidas circa 1938, the signed 17 jewel movement is housed in a German silver hall-marked snap-back case. The watch features a 30-minute register; the luminous dial has the outer chapter ring calibrated in fifths of a second, while the minute ring is marked with 24-hour numerals in red. The rear of the case bears the engraved Nazi national emblem and "Artl. 5551" issue number. **Value** *£250-£300*

Split chronograph watches have extra complications to the mechanical 17 jewel movement, in order to provide dual timing facilities. They operate like any ordinary stop watch, with both central hands running simultaneously as one. However, when the large button on the left of the winder is depressed one of the hands stops while the other continues to run. The operator can then make a note of the interim timing, and when the large button is depressed again this hand will rejoin the other. Both hands can be stopped by pressing down the winding crown, and a subsequent depression will reset the timer. This example of the split chronograph was issued to the Royal Air Force, as indicated by the crowned "A.M." mark and "6B" code. The enamel dial is dated "36" and the outer ring is calibrated in degrees.

Value *£40-£50*

This Royal Navy issue No.4 Pattern split chronograph pocket watch has an unsigned movement,
but may well have been made by Lemania, circa
1939. This watch is basically identical to those procured by the Air Ministry, although the Royal Air
Force issue models had a 17 jewel specification as
opposed to the Royal Navy's 15 jewel requirement.
Note again the style of the broad arrow found on
Royal Navy issue timepieces.
Value *£30-£40*

Waltham's Admiralty No.6 Pattern stop watches were designed circa 1940, for a specific purpose: they were calibrated to measure a distance of up to 5,000 yards over a maximum six-seconds interval. These watches were used in conjunction with the "Asdic" sonar apparatus aboard anti-submarine warships. Sound passes through seawater at approximately 1,650 yards per second (four times faster than through air). The Asdic operator started the timer on the emission of the sonar "bleep", the sound wave being reflected back from the target object, so travelling over twice

the distance in twice the time necessary to compute
the range of the submarine. The watch was therefore
calibrated to register a speed of half that of sound
through water, the scale showing approximately 830
yards per second, so eliminating the cumulative error.
Comparison of successive readings, and the direction-
finding capability of the Asdic apparatus, enabled the
range, speed and course of the U-boat to be plotted,
and depth charges could be primed to explode at the
correct depth. The screw back of each watch bears the
issue number and naval broad arrow property mark.
Value £35-£45

Strictly speaking this "Mark XV disk speed indicator" is not a timepiece in the normal sense. Instead of measuring the passage of time, this precision instrument records the number of revolutions made by, for example, a spinning propeller shaft on board a ship. Made by Jaeger in the USA during 1942, the movement contains a balance wheel mechanism resembling that of a normal watch. When the plunger to the left of the spindle is pressed, this gives sufficient impetus to the balance wheel to allow it to run (tick) for approximately 10 seconds. During this running time the user holds the spindle against a rotating shaft to record the number of revolutions made. Whether the spindle rotates in a clockwise or anticlockwise direction will make no difference to the fact that the indicating hand will only travel clockwise. The dial of this gauge is fully luminous, for use in the often dark environment of a ship's engineroom. A small metal plate has been riveted to the rear of the case identifying the gauge as being the property of the US Navy-Bureau of Ordnance.

Value *£60-£80*

The triangular emblem seen on the 30-minute register on the black dial of this Kriegsmarine pocket chronograph watch was used as the trademark for the German watch company Dugena of Darmstadt. The 17 jewel movement is unsigned, but has been identified as made by the Swiss company Lemania, circa 1941. The tough nickel case has a screw back, which suggests that the watch was probably intended for sea duties. The dial, the centre seconds hand and the indicator on the 30-minute register have all received a heavy coating of phosphorescent paint. Even the graduated chapter ring has been given a silver reflective finish, making the watch easily readable in dark conditions.
Value *£250-£280*

Made by Hanhardt circa 1942, this gunnery watch features a chronograph operated by the stop/start and reset pusher situated at 11 o'clock, with a 30-minute recording facility. The outer chapter ring is divided and numbered at five-second intervals, and each one-second unit is further graduated in fifths. A telemetric scale has also been added in red around the inside of the seconds chapter ring. This watch was clearly made for artillery range finding use. The nickel-plated brass outer case has an embossed checkered finish, perhaps as much for a secure grip in cold and wet as for decoration. The centre disc was at one time stamped with the Kriegsmarine eagle and swastika over M; however, this watch has been "deNazified" either by the French Navy – who used quantities of captured German equipment – or by its individual finder. **Value** *£250-£300*

This otherwise normal two-button chronograph wristwatch has been adapted by the maker, Optima, circa 1940. During construction at the factory they deliberately failed to fit the hour and minute wheels (together with the associated hands) to their 17 jewel movement, which would have given the watch its usual time-telling ability. A plainer dial than would be expected has been used on this piece, recording only the elapsing seconds totalling a period of 30 minutes; the 30-minute register is in red. Interestingly, a "shock-resist" device has been fitted to the balance. The back of this gold-plated watch is engraved with the designation "Pattern 3169" together with the Royal Navy pattern of broad arrow. Other versions of this watch, frequently made by Pierce, may also be encountered, most often with Army issue marks.
Value *£50-£60 (Optima and Pierce)*

This Pringle Mark II stop watch was issued to the Royal Artillery, circa 1940, though it bears an engraved "2 COY" mark (one would expect an artillery watch to be identified to a troop or battery?). The movement incorporates a balance wheel that oscillates at a rate of 10 times per second. This is twice the speed of the average timepiece, and consequently the centre hand makes one revolution of the dial every 30 seconds. Damage to this most vulnerable component, the balance - or more correctly, the staff upon which the balance wheel pivots - renders the watch useless. It would have to be returned to a qualified watchmaker for repair; and spare parts might be in short supply or unavailable when required. Ingeniously, then, two spare staffs were included with each Pringle stop watch supplied, and can be found located inside the watch itself beneath a special compart within the movement.

Value *£25-£30*

Army issue chronograph wristwatches, such as this example circa 1940, are scarce. The complexities of this watch, which not only has time-keeping abilities but also includes a mechanism to operate the integral interval timer, create added expense - always anathema to the British procurement authorities. Often it was considered more economical to supply two timepieces: an ordinary wristwatch, plus an additional stop watch. Nevertheless, this example, which has an unsigned 17 jewel

movement, obviates the need for the second timepiece, freeing the hands of the user. The copper coloured dial incorporates a telemetric scale, particularly useful in determining the range of, e.g., an enemy artillery position. The markings on the snap-on back denote that the watch is capable of timing intervals to an accuracy of one fifth of a second. Such watches were issued to the Army's Air Observation Post crews.

Value *£175-£200*

The bureaucratic preference for issuing both a watch and a stop watch on grounds of economy means that chronograph wristwatches issued to the British forces in the Second World War are very scarce. This particular example of a double-button chronograph was made by Pierce. It was issued to the Royal Air Force in 1943, and features a tachometric scale on the outside of the dial, used to calculate ground speed. The snap-back case is engraved "A.M.", "2836/43.", "6B." **Value** *£175-£225*

Longines complemented their range of precision navigational instruments by making a special chronograph wristwatch with "fly-back" centre seconds, circa 1940; this example has a Longines calibre 12.68Z 17 jewel movement in a nickel snap-back case. This model provided a hacking feature whereby, on a full depression of the pusher, the centre seconds hand returned to zero (12 o'clock); on release of the pusher its motion would resume. The benefits of this feature are numerous, depending on the tasks to hand. Although it is not confirmed, it is believed that this particular wristwatch was the property of the US Navy. It was issued to an individual whose name,"CAPT. W. BONNETTE", appears on the back.

It is likely that Captain Bonnette synchronised his wristwatch against the ship's chronometer before going on duty, perhaps in preparation for using his sextant in making astronomical calculations. Another use of this facility would be in calculating distances from the telemetric scale: the zeroed seconds hand could be started at the point of observing, say, the distant muzzle flashes from an enemy warship. As sound of the gunfire was heard, Captain Bonnette could depress the pusher halfway, stopping the seconds hand; the distance of the enemy warship could then be read directly from the watch.

This pattern of Longines wristwatch was also issued to the US Lighthouse Service for use in conjunction with Distance Finding Stations. During poor visibility at sea, the DFS would transmit a radio signal at regular intervals. Any passing ship would sound its foghorn in unison with the radio signal. On hearing the audible horn the lighthouse crew would rapidly calculate the distance of the ship from their location, using the fly-back seconds hand to monitor the time differential between the radio signal and the audible horn.

Value *£600-£700*

Heuer were quick to seize upon the sales potential that their connections with the Swiss Army might generate, when they produced this advertisement in the 1940s.

Hanhardt made a single-button chronograph wristwatch for the Wehrmacht, circa 1940. Although the Hanhardt was built to exacting standards, it nevertheless represented an economical alternative when compared with the Glashutte wrist chronograph. Used by all sections of the armed forces, but mainly associated with the Luftwaffe, the Hanhardt chronograph was only property-marked when in service with the Kriegsmarine, who stamped the screw back with a small eagle emblem reminiscent of a Waffenampt mark, over "M". Later a double-button version was introduced, which after the war continued in commercial manufacture well into the 1950s. (Courtesy Kent Sales)
Value £450-£500

This splendid Luftwaffe chronograph wristwatch was made by Lancet, circa 1940. The top button operates the chronograph mechanism in the 17 jewel movement, by starting, stopping and if necessary restarting the central sweeping seconds hand. The lower button is used to reset the movement. The complicated black dial incorporates two scales. A telemeter, calibrated in kilometres per hour, runs around the circumference of the dial; a tachometer, seen spiralling about the centre, is used to measure ground speed. Perhaps most interesting on this particular example, however, is the unit identification stamped on to the back of the snap case: "Kampfgeschwader 53, 11 Staffel". The Luftwaffe bomber wing KG53 was awarded the honour title "Condor Legion" and the lineage of the Spanish Civil War bomber squadron K88. Equipped with Heinkel He111 bombers, KG53 was active over England during the Battle of Britain, and later served on the Russian Front. (Courtesy D.Penny) **Value** *£500-£600*

Glashutte established itself as the centre of German watch production when, in the 1930s, the "Tutima" became the first wristwatch to be completely built in that country at the Uhrenroh-Werke-Fabrik (Urofa). Just before the outbreak of the Second World War Tutima also produced a fine wrist chronograph (identified by the "T" trademark) which immediately won acceptance by the military authorities. This double-button chronograph, with its 21 jewel movement, was to serve primarily with the Luftwaffe, and as such it does not have any issue markings. The Kriegsmarine also received a quantity of these timepieces, which can easily be identified by the eagle and swastika over "M". Following the end of the war Glashutte found itself in East Germany where, under the auspices of the Communist regime, watch production continued. Very similar chronographs were produced, using Urofa's original tooling, by the new company, Moscauer Uhrenfabrik, Kirow-Werke. These post-war chronographs are dated on the movement, e.g. "49r." for 1949 rok (year).
Value £900-£1,200 (Tutima)
£300-£350 (Moscauer Uhrenfabrik)

Aircraft, such as the Lancaster bomber, carried a stop watch fixed in an aperture of the instrument panel in the cockpit. This allowed the pilot to monitor his flight progress without constant reference to the navigator. The timer also acted as a back-up to a number of alternative instruments. In the event of their being put out of action the stop watch could perform the function of a rate-of-turn indicator, assisted by the 360 degree graduations around the dial; or a fuel management system. This particular example, dated to 1943, is coded "6B/221", indicating that it is of a "substitute" standard; i.e. this 7 jewel stop watch was not intended for seriously precise navigational use. **Value** *£20-£25*

Waltham manufactured fifteen variations of their 16 size, 9 jewel stop watch. In the main these differed only in the dial design and in the rapidity of the balance oscillation, ranging from five to an amazing 100 beats per second (360,000 balance oscillations per hour). In England it was the Admiralty which purchased the bulk of the Waltham stop watches; however, this example of a standard one-fifth-second timer, where the centre hand makes one revolution per minute, was supplied to the artillery, circa 1944. To the pilots of the US Army Air Forces and the US Navy's Bureau of Aeronautics this pattern of watch was the Type A-8, used to calculate ground speed. Type A-8s may also be encountered fitted with a 1/30 second timer, which has the dial track divided into ten seconds.

In the 1950s the French Navy and Air Force received their first deliveries of chronograph wristwatches. These were supplied by either Auricoste Breguet or Vixa, and were designated as the Type 20. A number of these were also procured by the Moroccan and Argentinian air forces. During the 1960s the cost of repairing and maintaining these chronographs was becoming prohibitive, and the spares for the Valjoux, Lemania or Hanhardt movements used in their manufacture were virtually exhausted. Consequently, a new Type 21 was introduced; this example, supplied by the Dodane company circa 1968, used the most modern 17 jewel Valjoux movement. The double-button facility allowed the chronograph to be started, stopped and if necessary restarted during the recording of the intervals. Another useful feature of this watch is the rotating bezel, calibrated from 1 to 12 hours in an anti-clockwise sequence. This can be used by the pilot as an aide memoire during the countdown of hours leading up to an event. The screw back shows evidence of three inspection dates prefixed "FG" (Fin Garantie), the earliest being 1969.
Value *£200-£300*

Lemania chronograph wristwatches have been chosen by a number of European air forces as suitable for issue to aircrew. Several different models became available circa 1945-1965, offering a variety of designs and functions. The earliest pattern has a white dial and only a single button; this was used by the Royal Navy and in particular by the pilots of the Fleet Air Arm. These watches are engraved with "H.S.9" and broad arrow marks. Later a black dial was introduced, and variants

could be acquired with either single- or double-button chronograph facilities. Regardless of the type, all models use Lemania's 17 jewel movements, which may be fitted with Incabloc shock protection. This particular example dating from 1956 has the Royal Air Force "6BB" prefix to the NATO issue number engraved to the back of the waterproof case.

Yet another offering in the Lemania range is the single-button "fly-back" model dating from circa 1960. The centre seconds hand on the "fly-back" wristwatch zeros itself when the single pusher is depressed, while the winding crown is simultaneously pushed out into the hand-setting mode. Once set to the correct time the watch is restarted by pushing the winding crown home. These "fly-back" watches were chosen by the Royal Swedish Air Force. (Courtesy Kent Sales)
Value *£250-£350*

In the 1970s the designers at Porsche produced a classic chronograph wristwatch aimed at the world of motorsport. Subsequently NATO expressed their interest in what was considered to be not only a rugged and dependable timepiece, but also a status symbol for the officers and select personnel who would be issued with one. NATO agreed a contract with the manufacturers and the Porsche "Military" chronograph was launched, differing only cosmetically from the original commercial design. Both models used the same 17 jewel Lemania movement, which was housed in a stainless steel case. The case, complete with the metal bracelet, was made non-reflective by a chemical process which turned the watch black. At this time the Royal Navy were also considering the purchase of Porsche chronographs, and a small batch were obtained for evaluation; these were marked "ROYAL NAVY" on the dial. A red circular symbol containing the letters "3H" was also printed on the dial, identifying the use of the element Tritium.

This marking conformed to military specification concerning the use of a radioactive source in the manufacture of the product; it stood for "Hydrogen 3", having a radioactive half-life of 12.5 years. For this batch commercial grade stainless steel watch cases, with an attractive satin finish, were used. Although these watches proved to be popular they exceeded the Royal Navy's requirements and regrettably proved to be too costly for the Senior Service's comparatively tight budget. However, news of this successful military timepiece was soon spreading, and orders for the Porsche chronograph were placed by the Swiss Army, the United Arab Emirates Air Force and the US 23rd Tactical Fighter Wing - the "Flying Tigers". The illustration is taken from the original user's instruction/specification sheet which accompanies the military chronograph wristwatch. **Value** _£450-£650 (NATO), £800-£900 (RN)_

Chronograph wristwatches made by CWC were issued to pilots and navigators in all branches of the British forces from circa 1974 to 1984. Hamilton also produced an identical model using the same 17 jewel Valjoux ebauche. All these models had twin pushers for starting, stopping, restarting or resetting the chronograph's centre seconds hand; the 30-minute register and a subsidiary seconds dial were also standard features. Late models supplied by Precista had a hacking device incorporated in the movement, which allowed the subsidiary seconds hand to be synchronised against a time signal.

Value *£200-£220 (CWC),*
£220-£250 (Hamilton, Precista)

Seiko currently manufacture the latest quartz chronograph wristwatch issued to airmen throughout the British armed forces. The first chronographs, as illustrated (maker's name in 12 o'clock position), appeared circa 1983 and remained unchanged for the next decade. The black luminous dials feature three subsidiary registers including continuous elapsing seconds, minutes, and fractions of a second down to one-tenth. Quartz technology also allows the user to make interim timings, so that two simultaneous events can be monitored, by virtue of the "lap time" facility. The most recent Seiko chronograph (maker's name at 3 o'clock) differs very little from the original NATO issue model, the main differences being in the layout of the subsidiary registers and the addition of a calendar.

An earlier chronograph wristwatch supplied to the RAF by Seiko was fitted with a bright yellow dial. These were specifically intended for issue to Vulcan bomber aircrews, most of whom had to work under particularly dark ambient conditions entombed deep inside the airframe; tests showed that the yellow colour provided the best contrast between the dial and hands.

Value *£120-£150*

Several days after the outbreak of the Gulf War, a group of news reporters were holed up in a Tehran hotel. A soldier unexpectedly hurried into the foyer, and made an excited announcement; then he produced a bag of watches and began to distribute them among the amazed foreigners - the idea seems to have been that the Iranians were claiming to have taken them from downed Iraqi pilots. In fact some 130 Iraqi aircraft fled into Iran, preferring internment to facing the Coalition airforces; these watches were presumably taken from their pilots. They bore the property marks of the Iraqi Air Force in both English and Arabic; and consisted of a variety of Breitling chronographs from the series known as the "NAVITIMER". Early examples were from the mid-1970s range with automatic movements, but this example was one of the most modern, dating from circa 1990. Known as the Navitimer 3000, the movement incorporates both analogue and digital displays, offering an array of

functions as well as high precision timekeeping.
The complicated bezel is actually a logarithmic
slide rule which can be used by the pilot to make
his pre-flight calculations, e.g. working out the
amount of fuel required, fuel burn rate, flying
time, flying speed, as well as a host of other
conversion functions. (Courtesy J.King)
Value *£300-£350*

SPECIAL FORCES & DIVER'S WRISTWATCHES

THE WATCH THAT FLEW OVER EVEREST

In their sensational flight over Everest, all members of the Houston Expedition were equipped with Rolex Oyster Watches. The following extract is from the official record:—

"Came the matter of watches of which any number were submitted for our approval. We wanted a watch that would tell the truth about time, a watch of lasting accuracy, and one that would go if we took it up to the stratosphere or deep down in the sea, a watch that would operate under all conditions . . .

Many were called but only one was chosen, the Rolex, *and it did all we asked of it.*

Stainless from £7 7s.

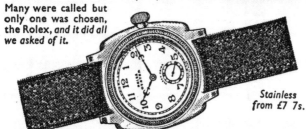

ROLEX "OYSTER"

DUST-PROOF · WATERPROOF · ANTI-MAGNETIC
27 World Records for Accuracy

The Oyster Watch is an indispensable part of an Officer's Equipment

Sold and Serviced by Leading Jewellers throughout the World

WRITE FOR ILLUSTRATED BOOKLET

ROLEX WATCH Co. Ltd.(*H. Wilsdorf, Managing Director*)
GENEVA · LONDON · PARIS
LONDON OFFICE: 40/44 HOLBORN VIADUCT, E.C.1

In 1935 Rolex placed this advertisement in the British military publication Field Service Regulations, claiming that their Oyster wristwatch was "an indispensable part of an Officer's Equipment".

Officine Panerai were an Italian company which specialised in acquiring technical and mechanical equipment, including watches, on behalf of the armed forces. If Panerai were unable to supply the military with equipment to meet a particular specification they would adapt and improve upon existing models. This is what happened in 1939, when the Italian Navy approached them with a request for a waterproof diver's wristwatch for issue to their frogmen teams - an area in which Italy was to lead the world early in the Second World War.

Originally a Rolex Oyster without any seconds hand was used in a large cushion-shaped case complete with Rolex's patented screw-down winding crown. This unfortunately proved to be the watch's Achilles heel; when new the seal in the winder was completely effective against partial sea immersion, but continuous daily use of the winder caused it to deteriorate, and watches subsequently failed when subjected to greater pressure at depth. Panerai set about designing a special clamp which fitted over the winding crown, subjecting the winder to direct pressure and creating an excellent case-to-crown seal; this allowed the watches to operate to a maximum depth of 30 meters. To reduce the cost of these watches Panerai also used an Angelus movement, which can be identified by the presence of a subsidiary seconds hand in the 9 o'clock position. When these diver's watches left Officine Panerai they were packaged with two other instruments, a depth gauge and a compass.

The Egyptian government subsequently approached Panerai to supply waterproof watches for issue to their commando units. For this contract Panerai worked on the sound theory that if the watch was wound on fewer occasions the seal would require less frequent maintenance, and an eight-day Angelus movement was used. Illustrated from left to right are the original Officine Panerai Rolex waterproof wristwatch, two accompanying diving instruments (depth gauge above compass), and an Egyptian contract eight-day Angelus diver's wristwatch. Each is complete with the original leather strap. (Courtesy Christie's) **Value** *£1,200-£1,400 (Rolex), £700-£800 (Angelus), £850-£950 (eightday Angelus)*

In September 1944 the German battleship *Tirpitz*
was attacked and damaged in a daring raid by
Royal Navy miniature submarines. Following this
incident the Kriegsmarine set about improving
their underwater defences by instituting more regular inspection by frogmen of ship's hulls for signs
of sabotage. The frogmen were issued with these
oversized waterproof wristwatches with unusual
luminous dials, the top half of which is printed
with Roman numerals, and the lower half with
Arabic. This is a characteristic of Rolex watches;
and the small 15 jewel pocket watch movement,
although unsigned, has been attributed to the Swiss
maker Cortebert, who are known to have supplied
Rolex with ebauches. Another Rolex patent which
has been incorporated in this watch is the screw-
down waterproof winding crown. All in all this
watch is something of a hybrid; its originality is
not in dispute, and it represents an interesting
marriage of various patents and designs.
(Courtesy P. Hockey)
Value *£800-£1,000*

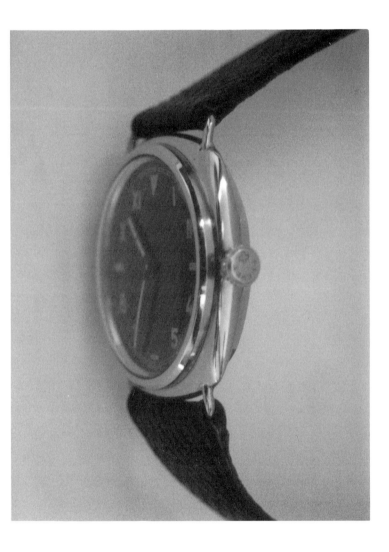

In 1943 the first Naval Combat Demolition Teams were formed, drawn primarily from volunteers serving with the US Naval Construction Battalions (the "Sea Bees") and originally working in the Mediterranean; expansion to the Pacific theatre brought a change of designation to Underwater Demolition Teams (UDTs). The UDTs' mission was to clear beach approaches of mines and any other obstacles in preparation for amphibious assault landings. To aid the frogmen in these tasks a special waterproof wristwatch was developed by Hamilton, using their Model 987S movement encapsulated in a special waterproof case. This featured a protective cap which screwed down to seal in the winding crown. Effective to a working depth of 50 feet, these watches allowed the frogmen to monitor their air supply.

Later, in the 1950s, Elgin introduced a new movement to their list of military grades. This 17 jewel Grade 647 was used in the manufacture of their UDT diver's wristwatch, as illustrated here, which resembled the earlier Hamilton. The back of this watch is stamped "USN Bu Ships". During the waterproof testing of these watches they were placed into a container and pressurised. They were then submerged in water and, if any air bubbles were seen to escape from any of the seals which surrounded the glass, case back and winding crown, the watch was rejected.
(Courtesy Sotheby's)
Value *£300-£350 (Hamilton), £250-£300 (Elgin)*

The US Navy UDTs survived the end of the Second World War, and went on to acquire a special combat operations role "above high water mark" during the Korean War. As part of President Kennedy's expansion of US unconventional warfare capability, in 1962 the existing UDT Teams 1 and 2 were subsumed into the new SEAL Teams 1 and 2 - the term "SEALs" referring to their ability to be inserted by sea, air or land. The specialist work of the SEALs called for a new breed of diver's wristwatch, able to operate at a depth of at least 165 feet. Automatic movements were mandatory to avoid the danger of the watch running down. Rotating bezels were also fitted, to act as a reference for the diver when monitoring air supplies and decompression stages.

In the late 1970s the SEALs were issued with this Benrus Type II Class A wristwatch. Manufactured to meet military specification MIL-W-50717, these watches were tested to depths of 495 feet. Another version of this watch was also introduced, differing only in that the dial had conventional numerals. The Benrus watch has also been supplied to Army Special Forces, Army Rangers and the Central Intelligence Maritime Units.
Value *£150-£170*

Rolex won fame for their waterproof Oyster wristwatch when, in 1926, Mercedes Gleitze swam the English Channel wearing one. In 1940 the Royal Navy acquired a small number of these Oyster watches for issue to its divers; these were engraved with the broad arrow and "H.S.10" code, and have subsequently become known, erroneously, as the Rolex "Army model". The illustrated wristwatch is the modern equivalent, the Rolex "Submariner". Issued to members of the Royal Marines Special Boat Squadron, it is engraved with the broad arrow on the Oyster back, together with a Royal Navy stores number, serial number and 1974 date. It differs from the civilian model in that the dial bears the obligatory encircled "T" emblem and the case has fixed strap lugs. This example is fitted with the later Mercedes hands; earlier pieces had an hour hand shaped as a stubby diamond. The dial states that the watch is waterproof to a depth of 200 metres, at which point the watch and diver would be subjected to pressures of 20 kilograms per square centimetre.

Value *£1,200-£1,500*

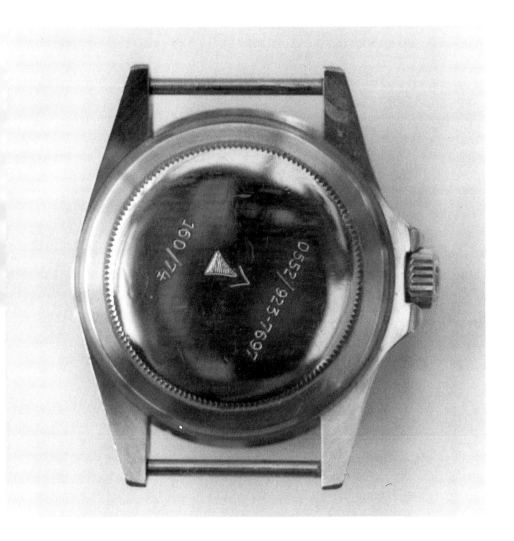

This Omega Seamaster 300 was issued to Royal
Navy divers circa 1970. As well as bearing the issue
marks, the back of the watch is engraved "Certified
High Pressure Waterproof". Unlike its commercial
counterpart this watch has been fitted with heavy
duty "fixed" strap bars.
Value *£270-£300*

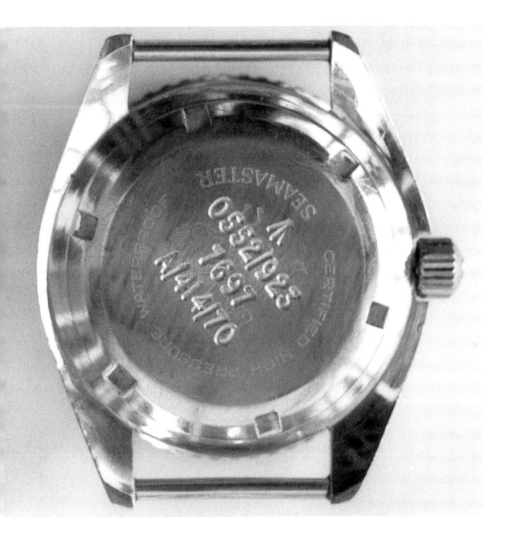

The life of a diver depends very directly on an
accurate and reliable timepiece, and not every
wristwatch is suited to this application. Obviously,
diver's watches must be waterproof even under the
considerable pressures encountered at the operating
depth. Secondly, the diver must be able to trust his
watch implicitly - not only to tell the time
accurately, but never to stop working; therefore an
automatic movement is the preferred choice, the
movement of the wearer activating the watch's
rotor, which automatically winds the mainspring.
The dive must be completed in plenty of time to
allow for the diver's ascent to be properly
sequenced, with decompression stages at various
depths to prevent the onset of the crippling
blood/gas condition known as "the bends". For
legibility in murky waters the dial on this Precista
diver's watch is marked with luminous rectangular
batons on each quarter, and circular marks at the
five-minute divisions in between. The 25 jewel
movement is of high quality. The back of the
stainless steel case bears the "0552" numerical
prefix to the stores number and is dated to 1981.
Value *£120-£150*

The CWC company supplied the Royal Navy with this quartz diver's wristwatch during the 1980s; obviously, it is important for the battery to be checked and changed on a regular basis to prevent failure during an underwater operation. These latest watches also incorporate a new safety feature. Unlike those on earlier divers' watches, the rotatable bezel is only permitted - by a ratchet - to turn anticlockwise; therefore, should the bezel be accidentally moved, the wearer who is using the bezel as a marker set to a pre-determined time may surface early, but will not overstay his time at depth.

Value *£60-£80*

In order for the RM Special Boat Squadron to perform their demanding role as the Royal Navy's elite
underwater insertion reconnaissance force, a special
purpose wristwatch was developed for them by
CWC circa 1995. Superficially this resembles the
standard diving watch produced by the same company. However, the SBS issue model has a high
specification quartz movement fitted, plus a day
and date calendar. A durable matt black phosphate
finish eliminates any possibility of tell-tale reflec-
tions when in the presence of the enemy. The back
of the case is engraved with the broad arrow and
"0552"-prefixed stores reference numbers. This
example is in unissued condition.

Value *£250-£300*

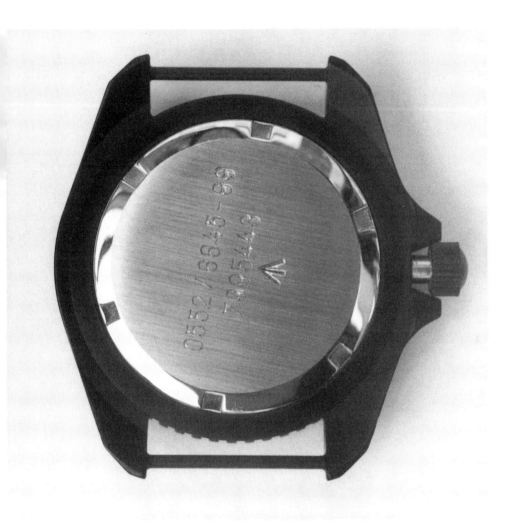

MANTLEPIECE, WALL & AIRCRAFT CLOCKS

Royal Air Force clocks of this pattern first appeared circa 1929 and continued in production until 1939. Each clock has a well-proportioned oak case which houses an eight-day Elliott fusee movement. These movements are frequently dated on the lower part of the back plate; this particular clock does not have a date stamped onto the movement, but can be dated to 13 February 1933 from the original inventory label which remains on the base of the case. Interestingly, this label also bears the station details, which are recorded as *HMS Flowerdown* -presumably this Royal Navy shore establishment was home to the RAF during the heyday of the flyingboat. It is only the early Elliott clocks which have the RAF winged crest engraved on to the 5.5-inch silvered dial.
Value *£280-£300*

Later examples of the Elliott mantelpiece clock, such as this 1938-dated version, only have the crowned RAF wreath engraved on the dial. These were typically used in sergeant's messes. While examples vary in the manner of their case marking, this clock exhibits a standard array of Air Ministry property stamps and manufacturer's details on the oak case. Most famously, an example of this clock may be found on the mantelpiece in the hallway of 10 Downing Street, the Prime Minister's residence. Larger RAF clocks by Elliott, with 7-inch dials and bigger oak cases with a flat, rather than an apex top may also be encountered from the prewar period. **Value** *£220-£250*

In 1936, following much research and development into "radio direction and range finding", Royal Air Force Fighter Command conducted their annual exercise between Bawdsey and Biggin Hill to test the validity of the new top secret "radar" equipment as an early warning "control and reporting" (C&R) system, working in conjunction with the Observer Corps and reporting to a central control staff in an RAF Group Operations Room. Information received by the Group Ops Room concerning the height, bearing and strength of approaching hostile aircraft would be plotted on large table maps. Group would then alert the most appropriate of its subordinate Sector Operations Rooms, who would take charge of the local aerial activity once their squadrons had been "scrambled". The theory of C&R proved a success in practice; and by the outbreak of war the Royal Air Force had the best-organised early warning network in the world, uniquely served by the "Chain Home" radar stations along the coast. Without this well-integrated system the outcome of the Battle of Britain - finely balanced as it was - would have been very different.

Work in the Group Ops Rooms was hectic. Numerous incoming messages had to be sorted, prioritised and disseminated at speed; late information could send a precious squadron of Hurricanes or Spitfires looking for hostile targets on bearings and at altitudes long since vacated by an enemy raid, which in August 1940 would often be heading for the fighter stations themselves. An instant method of weeding out stale information from current reports was therefore devised.

All fresh reports would be colour-coded either red, yellow or blue according to the time when they were received, using a special clock which had its dial painted with this trio of colours at five-minute intervals in succession around the dial (in this photograph the segment between 12 and 1 o'clock is red, that between 1 and 2 yellow, that between 2 and 3 blue, and so on in the same sequence). The colour indicated by the minute hand at the time when the report was received would be the colour code given to the message.

For example, during the height of the Battle of Britain, No.11 Group situated at Uxbridge might receive a message from Hornchurch, one of the Group's Sector stations, stating "503 Squadron reports Enemy Sighted". Should the clock's minute hand be in the red, that report would be coded as "red". Once the minute hand had passed on through the yellow segment, the Controller would realise that the information was now some five minutes old. Once the time on the clock had gone beyond the blue and into the next red segment, 503 Squadron's status could no longer be considered accurate. However, if in the meanwhile Hornchurch contacted Group with the message "503 Squadron calling, Enemy Engaged", the information board would be updated with the current colour of the time, ensuring that the Controller remained in full command of the developing battle. More fighters could then be scrambled to intercept the enemy at 503's reported location. This mass of information was recorded in the Operations Room on the Squadron State boards situated opposite the Controller's podium. The Sector clock, an Elliott eight-day fusee wall clock, was positioned on the wall alongside the state board for easy reference. An identical clock would hang on an adjacent wall to act as a "back-up" should one become inoperative.

While the Elliott clocks were robust and capable of delivering fine accuracy, their pendulum-driven movements were easily disrupted, which inevitably led to stoppages should the clock be knocked from its level position - not an uncommon mishap during air raids. Consequently, an alternative clock was introduced circa 1941. The new Operations Room clock (as illustrated here) was made by Smiths, employing their industrial grade "Astral" movement which was operated by a lever escapement, protected beneath a metal cover at the top of the movement. Due to the use of a lever escapement the Smiths clock could be moved around without detriment to its accuracy. The King's Crown Air Ministry mark can be seen on the movement together with a 1942 date.

Value *£700-£800 (Smiths) £1,000-£1,200 (Elliott)*

A good, clean, genuine example of a Royal Air Force wall clock, circa 1939. The pendulum movement is stamped F.W. Elliott; however, it does not contain a fusee to maintain the uniform distribution of the mainspring's energy while it winds down. Nevertheless, these utility office clocks can still achieve excellent levels of accuracy, and unsurprisingly they were used in many government establishments (without RAF marks); consequently a great number have survived. Today the original RAF issue clocks sell at a premium, and it is not surprising that unscrupulous individuals add the RAF crest to the plain dial clocks in an attempt to pass them off as Air Ministry prop-

erty. Although this faking is sometimes crude, it can be skilfully accomplished - but regardless, it can be detected by close examination. An original dial should be even and flat; this is because it has been silk screen printed in one process. The forgery has the crest applied (hand painted) onto an otherwise completed dial, and the fresh crest will be slightly raised in relief when compared with the numerals. An original oak case is also likely to bear some other proprietary marking. In this instance, only the faint trace of a mis-stamped crowned "A.M." mark exists, confirming the clock's provenance.

Value *£350-£375*

Even the Navy, Army & Air Force Institution had their own personalised wall clocks; after all, most of the NAAFI's habitual clientele often had important reasons for keeping an eye on the time. These oak-cased clocks made by Smiths, circa 1940, have a lever escapement on a platform on top of the movement. The horizontal slot above "SMITHS" gives access to the balance regulating arm.
Value *£120-£140*

Known as a "time of trip" chronograph, this timepiece, made by Jaeger Le Coultre in 1939, incorporates two clocks within one. At the start of the flight the pilot sets the small "time of trip" register dial to zero hours (12 o'clock), together with the large fly-back centre seconds hand. Meanwhile, the larger dial carries on indicating the standard time. As the clock runs on the duration of the flight is automatically recorded: in this instance a flight time of 9 hours, 36 minutes and 10 seconds has been registered. This complicated clock was intended for use in long-range, e.g. bomber aircraft; but despite its intended application, the then-Squadron Leader Douglas Bader is one fighter pilot who is known to have fitted this type of clock on to the instrument panel of his Spitfire.
Value *£100-£120*

Cockpit clocks, such as this eight-day Mark II example by Smiths, dated 1944, were bolted to the cockpit instrument panels in a multitude of different aircraft types throughout the war. Being a late-war production timepiece, this example is housed in a Bakelite casing. The winding knob protrudes from the right side. A second, red pair of movable hands is also featured on the outside of the clock glass; these can be rotated manually to any position, and would have been used by the pilot as a visual reminder of his take-off time.
Value *£35-£45*

During the Second World War the German military authorities laid down strict regulations concerning the issue of timepieces; these dictated that the Kriegsmarine would have the overall responsibility for approving any requests for clocks or watches from the Heer, Luftwaffe and Waffen-SS. Any watches that required maintenance would again be returned to the Kriegsmarine for correction. Inventories were kept at the naval ports of Wilhelmshaven, Kiel and Gotenhafen, ensuring that each unit/ship maintained a strict complement of designated timepieces. This bulkhead clock, circa 1942, with its lockable waterproof bezel, is one of six that would have been carried on board a U-boat. Its outer case, of turned brass, contains an eight-day Junghans movement. Below the issue number "9241" on the silvered dial is the letter "N", denoting that the clock was used by the North Sea (Nordsee) fleet.
Value *£350-£400*

The radio room on board a warship used a special type of eight-day clock; this example was supplied to the Kriegsmarine by Junghans, circa 1942. A three-minute segment after every quarter on the dial has been painted blue. As the minute hand entered this phase of the dial the radio room would fall silent, and for the next three minutes the wireless operator listened out for any vital incoming messages, from the enemy or otherwise, that he might intercept. The dial is engraved with the Kriegsmarine eagle over "M"; the "O" seen below the serial number indicates that the clock was on board a ship serving with the Eastern (Osten) fleet. (Courtesy Kent Sales)
Value *£300-£400*

Following the occupation of the Channel Islands in 1940 the Kriegsmarine established their headquarters on the island of Guernsey. This clock, as the dial inscription suggests, was reputedly removed from the naval base at St.Peter's Port when the island was liberated in 1945. Made by Junghans circa 1942, the clock has a standard eight-day movement fitted into a pressed brass case. No effort has been made to waterproof this timepiece, which suggests that it was used in a shore establishment; such clocks would have been hung on the walls of virtually every office. The silver dial has large numerals with a smaller 24-hour time scale alongside. A subsidiary seconds dial is positioned just below the "slow-fast" regulator slot underneath the figure 24.

Value *£200-£250*

This Kriegsmarine clock, measuring approximately 70mm in diameter, would at one time have been mounted in a small, upright wooden case. These clocks were used in various locations both on board vessels and in shore establishments. They were intended as no more than room clocks, to be used for easy reference. Made by Junghans circa 1942, they have an eight-day movement. The "pull" to the right of the case allows the clock to be swung open to reveal a large knurled winder. Care must be taken with this type of clock, as the inner case which holds the ratchet and winding mechanism together is made of a cast alloy, which has frequently begun to disintegrate with age. Apart from their use as table clocks, it is likely that some may have been fitted directly into bulkheads or instrument panels.

Value *£130-£150*

When it came to the production of aircraft instruments, in particular cockpit clocks, Germany was already self-sufficient and did not need to look to the Swiss to make up any shortfall in production. Two companies, Junghans and Keinzle, dominated this market, and produced the clocks used in all aircraft, tanks, etc. during the Second World War. This particular example of an aircraft clock, circa 1940, was made by Junghans. The grey-painted alloy case houses the chronograph movement, which is activated by the oval button situated beneath the knurled winder. The minute register is calibrated for a maximum time span of only 15 minutes; however, the rotating bezel is marked in minutes and can be used to monitor the passage of longer intervals. The long lever which protrudes from beneath the right side of the clock engages and disengages the winding or hand-setting facility.

Value *£80-£100*

When the National Socialist party came to power in Germany in 1933 there was a widespread culture of demonstrative support for the regime. Various manufacturers were quick to appeal to the popular mood by exploiting the swastika emblem, still something of a novelty for many. This crude eight-day clock, made circa 1935, is just such an item. The black-painted wooden case displays a coloured inlay of the Nazi flag, and the hour hand also incorporates the image of the swastika. (Courtesy Kent Sales)

Value *£100-£120*

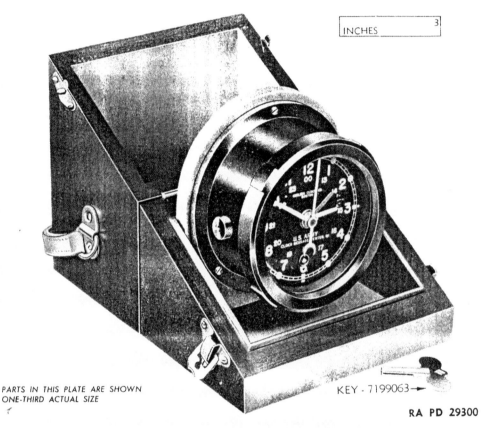

INCHES 3

KEY - 7199063 →

RA PD 29300

PARTS IN THIS PLATE ARE SHOWN
ONE-THIRD ACTUAL SIZE

Figure 201 — Message Center Clock M1 (Later Manufacture)

Figure 201 in the US manual TM 9-1575 illustrates the M1 Message Center Clock, the dial of which is marked "U.S. ARMY". These were made by the Chelsea Clock Company, circa 1941, for use by formation and unit HQs, artillery units, and any other message-sending branch of the armed forces. By reference to these clocks the precise time of incoming signals or despatches would be noted. The addition of the extra hour hand, which could be set independently, allowed the display of the time in another time zone. The M1 clock was stored in a wooden carry-case for ease and safety of transportation.

Value *£120-£150*

Known in military nomenclature as the Civil Date
Indicator Aeronautical (CDIA) clock, this particular example was manufactured by Waltham during
a production run that lasted from 1941 to 1944.
The 15 jewel 37 size movement employed is of the
eight-day type, which had first been developed in
1910 for the automobile industry; now, with a few
modifications, it was redesigned for use as an aircraft clock. Probably the most striking feature of
the CDIA clock is its 24-hour dial marked in white
and blue-green. The hour hand makes one orbit of
the dial in each 24-hour period; the time shown in
this photograph therefore translates into 1506
hours or 3.06pm. For every orbit completed by the
hour hand another indicator moves one position,
recording the passage of days against the central
blue-green chapter ring, which is marked from 1 to
31. A central sweep second hand is also included.
These clocks were secured by four screws to the
instrument panel of the aircraft cockpit. The clock
was wound by means of the winding knob situated
in the 15 o'clock position. The dial is marked
"CIVIL DATE" and a further inscription, not visible in the photograph, reads "WALTHAM U.S.
NAVY BU AERONAUTICS".
Value *£70-£80*

This inexpensive American-made bedside alarm clock, retailing to the troops at $1.65 and known as the "WARALARM", was of very basic construction; the dial was made of printed paper, and the black-finished outer casing was of pressed fibre. Nevertheless countless thousands of them were used, predominantly around air stations to wake military personnel.

Value *£15-£20*

Traditional Royal Air Force wood- or Bakelite-cased wall clocks, typical of the 1930s-40s, were superseded by mass produced moulded plastic clocks, such as this example dated 1953. Made by Smiths in England, the 7 jewel movements were the same as those used in dashboard clocks by the automobile industry. These office clocks were wound on a weekly basis, by means of the large knob seen protruding from the case below the 6 o'clock. The dial has the crowned Air Ministry mark.

Value *£35-£40*

GLOSSARY

Automatic. Mechanical movement with the ability to wind itself.

Balance Cock. The bridge, secured to the movement by a single screw at one end, that holds the balance wheel in place.

Balance Wheel. An oscillating wheel connected to the hair spring, used to regulate the time keeping ability of a watch.

Balance staff. The arbor or axis on which the balance wheel rotates.

Bezel. The grooved ring of a clock or watch case that contains the glass.

Borgel Case. An early form of waterproof watchcase, of monobloc design by Borgel.

Bow. The suspension ring joining the neck of a pocket watch.

Calibre. Term used by watch companies, to identify a particular model of watch movement.

Case. The reciptacle containing the movement.

Chapter. Roman or Arabic numerals marked around the circumference of the dial, usually identifying the hours.

Chaton. A metal ring into which a watch jewel is set, the chaton being either friction-fitted or held in the movement by screws.

Chronograph. A watch or clock with the capability of recording time intervals.

Chronometer. An exact time keeper.

Cylinder. A patented device for providing the impulse to the balance wheel

Deck Watch. A portable chronometer watch.

Detent. Term normally associated with marine chronometers, identifying an escapement which has been fitted with a detaining device, to detain or lock the escape wheel.

Escapement. The part of a watch movement that checks the energy supplied by the main spring and transfers it to the pendulum or balance wheel.

Ebauche. A movement in its raw state.

Fusee. A pulley device connected to the main spring barrel by a chain, which maintains a uniform release of power throughout the running duration of the clock or watch.

Gymbals. A suspension joint used to keep a marine chronometer level.

Hack Watch. A watch fitted with a device for interrupting the balance mechanism.

Hands. Orbiting indicators used to tell the time against the watch dial.

Incabloc. Patented spring device which allows the balance staff to withstand minor shock.

Isochronism. The ability of the balance wheel to rotate through various arcs of motion at a constant rate.

Jewel. A bearing made from precious or semi precious stone.

Lever. An improved device for providing the impulse to the balance wheel.

Master Timepiece. An exact timekeeper by which other watches can be set.

Micrometer Regulator. A movable regulator fitted to the balance cock, capable of fine adjustment by turning a finely threaded screw or similar arrangement.

Movement. All the working parts of the watch or clock.

Observation Watch. Watch used for navigation, reconnaissance or surveillance.

Positions, number adjusted for. The number of positions in which a watch has been tested and adjusted for isochronism, i.e. inverted, upright, on its side, etc.

Shock Resistant. A watch's to withstand minor impact without causing mechanical damage.

Sidereal Time. Time keeping system used in astronomy. It is calculated by the period of time taken for the Earth to make one rotation of its axis.

Solar Time. Method of timekeeping by monitoring the passage of the SUIT over the meridian.

Split Chronograph. A watch equipped with the facility to record time intervals of two simultaneous events.

Stop Watch. A watch used solo for recording a time interval.

Tachymetric Scale. A scale calculated to measure speed over a predetermined distance.

Telemetric Scale. A graduated scale used to determine the distance of an object or phenomenon from the observer.

Waterproof. The ability for a watch to prevent the ingress of water, even if fully immersed for short periods, but not at depth.

Water Resistant. The watch's partial ability to resist the ingress of water under normal conditions.